FROM
HELLO TO GOODBYE

Proactive Tips for Maintaining
Positive Employee Relations

SECOND EDITION

Christine V. Walters, J.D., MAS, SHRM-SCP, SPHR

FROM HELLO TO GOODBYE

Proactive Tips for Maintaining Positive Employee Relations

Society for Human Resource Management
Alexandria, Virginia | shrm.org

Society for Human Resource Management, India Office
Mumbai, India | shrmindia.org

Society for Human Resource Management
Haidian District Beijing, China | shrm.org/cn

Society for Human Resource Management, Middle East and Africa Office
Dubai, UAE | shrm.org/pages/mena.aspx

This publication is designed to provide accurate and authoritative information regarding the subject matter covered. It is sold with the understanding that neither the publisher nor the author is engaged in rendering legal or other professional service. If legal advice or other expert assistance is required, the services of a competent, licensed professional should be sought. The federal and state laws discussed in this book are subject to frequent revision and interpretation by amendments or judicial revisions that may significantly affect employer or employee rights and obligations. Readers are encouraged to seek legal counsel regarding specific policies and practices in their organizations.

This book is published by the Society for Human Resource Management (SHRM). The interpretations, conclusions, and recommendations in this book are those of the author and do not necessarily represent those of the publisher.

SHRM books and products are available on most online bookstores and through the SHRMStore at www.shrmstore.org.

The Society for Human Resource Management (SHRM) is the world's largest HR professional society, representing 285,000 members in more than 165 countries. For nearly seven decades, the Society has been the leading provider of resources serving the needs of HR professionals and advancing the practice of human resource management. SHRM has more than 575 affiliated chapters within the United States and subsidiary offices in China, India and United Arab Emirates. Visit us at shrm.org.

Cover Design	Katerina Cochran
Interior Design	Shirley E.M. Raybuck
Manager, Creative Services	James McGinnis
Manager, Book Publishing	Matthew Davis
Vice President, Editorial	Tony Lee

Library of Congress Cataloging-in-Publication Data

Walters, Christine V., author
    From Hello to Goodbye: Proactive Tips for Maintaining Positive Employee Relations/Christine V. Walters.
    ISBN 978-1-586-44447-1 (pbk. alk. paper); ISBN 978-1-586-44449-5 (epub); ISBN 978-1-586-44450-1 (eMobi); ISBN 9781586444488 (PDF)
    LCSH: Personnel management. | Performance standards. | Problem employees. | Employees--Dismissal of. LCC HF5549 .W337 2017 | DDC 658.3--dc23

Printed in the United States of America

SECOND EDITION

PB Printing   10 9 8 7 6 5 4 3 2 1   61.13508-2 | 17-0297

Table of Contents

Backword: Getting It Right from the Start

You've seen it happen time and time again, right? We work backwards. That is, we begin focusing on an employment relationship as it nears its end; e.g., when our employee is not performing as expected and we are thinking about letting him go. That's when your legal counsel or HR administrator asks the eternal question, "Do you have any documentation?" Then when you let the employee go you receive a charge from the U.S. Equal Employment Opportunity Commission (EEOC), or your state or local commission.

It is in that spirit that this book is written — to reflect not how this process should work but how it often happens: backwards. You may start at the end of the book, which is the beginning of the employment relationship, or start at the beginning of the book, which is the end of the employment relationship. Either way, when you finish this book, you will hopefully have some new insights, practical tips, and ideas for ensuring that the door does not hit you on the employee's way out.

There are just five things to consider as you read this book:

1. Those of you who know me know that my favorite answer for many questions is two words: "It depends." No strategy, practice, or procedure will work well in every situation or for every person. So keep in mind that this book is intended only to serve as a guide to offer tips for proactive practices, not the right answer for any particular situation.

2. For the reasons cited above and more, this book does not constitute the rendering of legal advice. You should contact your company's legal counsel for guidance on any particular employee situation.

3. The use of the pronoun he/him/his is sex neutral and applies to either sex or both.

4. We often hear about "best" practices. As you read this book, you will find that I refer to "proactive" practices. I am pleased to read the EEOC's current use of the term "Promising Practices." Because businesses vary so much in what, where, when, and how they do business, I find there are few "best" practices. I find there are, however, myriad proactive practices — and that is the focus of this book.

5. Make the most of this book. Each chapter closes with practical tips. Consider these as you review and update your company's policies, practices, and procedures. There are also myriad links and resources provided in the endnotes for you. It is my hope that this book can become a resource that you can use repeatedly.

1

When All Else Fails: Terminating the Employment Relationship

Well, here you are at the end of the employment relationship. You have coached, counseled, and attempted to correct, yet the employee's behavior is still not meeting expectations. Thus, you have concluded that it is time to terminate the employment relationship. So what are some final steps you should take to ensure you have dotted and crossed your proverbial i's and t's? Consider the following.

Pre-Termination Checklist

Use the following five questions as a pre-termination checklist. This can help in a variety of ways — from preparing your presentation for an unemployment insurance hearing to defending your action before a federal or state agency or local human relations commission, and, perhaps more importantly, helping to ensure consistent treatment of all employees who are in similar situations.

Forewarning
Are you able to describe when and how you set your standard or expectation for this particular employee? Or is this a case where your position is, "Aw, come on, everyone knows you are supposed to ..." or "Everyone knows you are not supposed to ..." While this might hold true for lying, cheating, and stealing (although certain actions of select political, business, and other leaders might lead one to conclude that *nothing* can be taken for granted), it is not the case for most performance standards. Take,

for example, excessive absenteeism or tardiness. I find this is a common standard that managers believe with all honesty and conviction that everyone shares and thus there is no need to define it. But, when discussing the matter with peers and colleagues, they regularly find that their expectations may not match those of their peers, including managers and supervisors in the same department, as well as across the organization. Try the following exercise with your management team, particularly those managers working in the same department. Ask them to write down on a sheet of paper their answer to the question, "How many unscheduled occurrences of absence in a six-month period do you consider to be excessive?" Then go around the room and have them answer one at a time while you record the answers. You can be pretty much guaranteed that you will find differences, sometimes vast, among their answers. Some may say three; some may say six. Now there may be very valid reasons for having different standards in different departments. For example, if I am an HR administrator in a hospital (which I was for nearly 10 years), it is likely that my attendance and punctuality standard for my HR staff would be different and possibly more lenient than the standard a director might have in a nursing unit for the direct care providers. Why? There is at least one valid business reason: The impact to business operations when my HR staff is late is less or at least potentially less than when a direct care provider is late or absent. There is no direct harm if a file is left unattended for some period of time. There may be dire harm if a patient is left unattended for any amount of time. So remember that what you take for granted as a reasonable expectation may not be shared by others; communicate your expectations from the beginning of the employment relationship.

How? Consider developing a new employee orientation checklist list (see Chapter 7). When an employee does not meet your expectation, provide objective and specific examples of desired performance (see Chapter 3). And, throughout these processes, remember to document these activities (see Chapter 2), because only then will you be well positioned if and when the time comes to demonstrate how and when you provided the employee with forewarning of your expectation.

What if you find managers within the same department have different expectations? Talk about the differences and why they exist.

Are the rationales justified based on business need or are they subjective? For example, let's say there are three managers in the accounting department: one in accounts receivable (A/R), one in accounts payable (A/P), and one in payroll. Each supervises one to three employees. One manager believes an employee should have no more than six unscheduled absences in a six-month period; the second manager believes an employee should have no more than four unscheduled absences in a six-month period; and the third manager believes an employee should have no more than two unscheduled absences in a six-month period. The managers should focus on the impact that employee absences have on business operations, compare and contrast the impact, and understand why they have set different standards. The A/R manager may indicate that unscheduled absences have the potential to delay the collection of money from clients and customers, which reduces the company's cash-on-hand, which might impact its bond rating or leave less money available for investments and thereby reduce interest income. The A/P manager may indicate that unscheduled absences have the potential to delay payments to vendors, which may result in late fees or charges, causing unnecessary costs to the company. The payroll manager may indicate that unscheduled absences have the potential to delay the processing of payroll, which could result in fines if employees are not paid in a timely fashion, not to mention the bad employee morale that may be created. All three concerns are tied to business operations and are valid. They might not, however, justify such a broad difference in the expectation. Thus, the managers might work with human resources to determine what is the company's average absenteeism rate per employee and agree upon one standard that all three managers will use for the entire accounting department.[1]

Evidence

Do you have evidence to corroborate your position that the employee has failed to meet expectations? Evidence usually comes in one of three forms:

Employee's admission. Often an employee will admit to having done something incorrectly or inappropriately. But don't stop there. Asking, "Why?" can be a powerful inquiry; just knowing what an employee did may not be enough. Understanding why the employee did or failed to do something often opens doors to learning about systems, processes, training, communication, or other systems that need some fine tuning or are just not working. If that is the case, both you and the employee now have the opportunity to learn. You might establish a new training program or implement a new (or adjust an existing) policy or procedure. Sometimes, however, the employee does not admit to an error or omission despite evidence to the contrary. Thus, you will need to consider what other evidence you have to substantiate your claim.

Witnesses. You may have one or more witnesses who will report that they saw or heard or otherwise have knowledge of the alleged behavior. Having two or more witnesses is generally better than having just one witness. But what if you have just one witness and it becomes a matter of one employee's word against the other? Consider whether the witness would have any reasonable motive for fabricating the report. Does the employee have any reasonable motive for denying the allegation? This is where judgment comes into play. While it is subjective, you will need to determine whether it is more likely than not that the witness is telling the truth. Sometimes you may be left with a non-finding; that is, you cannot determine whether it is more likely that one employee is telling the truth over the other. In this instance, you might take this as an opportunity to meet with the employee to coach, counsel, educate, and/or reinforce a policy or expectation with regard to conduct or work performance. Document that meeting (see Chapter 2); if the matter should arise again, your documentation may help establish the likelihood that the employee has, in fact, engaged in the alleged conduct or failed to perform as expected or required. It will at least help establish the first element of forewarning and demonstrate that you did set the standard or expectation. The same could also be the case of multiple witnesses who may, on occasion, collude to create a story to get a coworker they dislike in trouble. Be open to considering these options. Often you have to conduct a credibility assessment. You may have to determine which story is more accurate. This is where seeking assistance from human resources or another management colleague can help. An objective set of eyes and ears may help you decipher the truth of the matter. If you don't have any witness(es) or the employee's own admission, don't give up yet. Try and find some tangible evidence.

Tangible evidence. You may have tangible evidence — such as time-clock punches, video recordings from security cameras, e-mail or voice mail messages, Internet logs, written notes, etc. — that will corroborate your allegation. If you have none of the above, you may want to reevaluate your impression or opinion of the employee's performance and ensure that you are not biased in any way. This does not mean you had any ill-intent; rather, sometimes we can be influenced by what we have heard about an employee's performance, attitude, conduct, etc. If you hear that an employee is initiating gossip about a coworker and there is suddenly a report of a rumor being spread around your department about a coworker, you might immediately assume that you know who started the rumor or gossip. Don't assume; get evidence to substantiate your position.

Proper Investigation

Have you conducted a proper investigation prior to making your final decision to terminate employment? Just because you have your evidence as listed above doesn't mean the case is closed. Perhaps one of the most important elements of conducting a proper investigation includes getting the employee's side of the story before you make your final decision with regard to any adverse employee action. It has happened more than once that an employee tells the story of being called into the manager's office and asked to give his side of the story regarding an incident and, after he does so, the manager then turns over a sheet of paper that was sitting on the manager's desk during the entire meeting. The sheet of paper turns out to be a written notice of corrective action, which the manager then issues to the employee. What message did the employee just receive? That action speaks volumes to the fact that it did not matter what the employee said; the manager had already made up his mind. Be open to explanations, even if the conduct is unacceptable. Take sleeping on duty as an example. I remember a situation in which a director came to human resources and wanted an employee fired for sleeping on duty. The employee had already received written, corrective action for sleeping on duty, and this was also in a direct patient care area so the potential impact in failing to respond to a patient could have had serious negative consequences. The director had done a good preliminary job of gathering evidence. The director produced statements from at least two coworkers who had observed the employee sleeping. When I suggested the director get the employee's side of the story, however, the director declined. The director's position was that there was no acceptable reason for sleeping on duty, and since the employee had already been warned once, termination was warranted. So, the employee was fired for sleeping on duty. The matter went through the grievance process and then to arbitration. The arbitrator reinstated the employee without back pay. Why? The arbitrator wrote that while he had reason to doubt the employee's veracity (the employee said she was not sleeping, only resting her eyes) he added that by the director's own admission she had failed to conduct a thorough investigation; she had failed to get the employee's side of the story before terminating the employee. What could be a reasonable excuse for sleeping on duty? Perhaps the employee had just been prescribed a new medication for a medical condition and the medication made her sleepy. Without getting that information first, you might have not only terminated the employee without knowing all the facts, you may also have a discrimination charge on your hands for failure to engage the employee in an interactive dialogue or provide reasonable accommodation under the Americans with Disabilities Act.

Lack of Discrimination

This element goes beyond what you may think when you hear the term "discrimination." It goes beyond legally protected classes such as age, race, religion, national origin, disability, sex, etc. It goes to the issue of equitable treatment. Ask yourself, "Is it your obligation as the employer to treat your employees equally or equitably?" Most likely the answer is the latter. You may not want to treat all your employees exactly the same or equally; you want to reward your top performers and provide incentives to those who go above and beyond. Likewise, you may not want to impose the same sanctions or penalties to employees who are not similarly situated or who have different situations. Take attendance and punctuality as a common example.

A key question is whether you have treated this employee the same as others who have been similarly situated. This is where we distinguish between equal treatment and equitable treatment. Let's say you are preparing to terminate an employee who has been coached, counseled, and received corrective action for excessive absenteeism, and who has now incurred a total of 10 separate and unscheduled occurrences in the last six months. So you might ask, has any other employee incurred 10 unscheduled occurrences in a six-month period and *not* been terminated? If your answer is "Yes" then your next step is to determine why you are treating two employees differently who appear to be similarly situated. Perhaps it is because they are not, in fact similarly situated. While both have incurred the same number of occurrences in the same period of time, the circumstances may not be the same. Imagine the first employee's absences were all related to the same reason, such as caring for a critically or terminally ill relative, and the employee has worked for you for several years and has an otherwise exemplary work record. The second employee's absences, however, have been for a variety of unrelated reasons, none of which are particularly unique or exigent, and this employee has worked for you for less than one year and is only a marginal performer. While the two situations appear on their face to be the same, the circumstances are quite different. In this case, issuing corrective action to the latter employee and not the former may be justified.

Penalty Meets the Offense

Finally, ask if termination is warranted; e.g., is it reasonable to expect that any lesser penalty would correct the behavior? If the employee has already been coached and counseled and has received corrective action on three prior occasions, then it may be unreasonable to expect that a fourth would make any difference. But when an employee has not been given at least one or perhaps two opportunities to correct the behavior, it might be reasonable to think that you could salvage the relationship, not to mention get a positive return on your investment (ROI) on the time and money you have invested in the recruitment, selection, hiring, and training of this employee.

Policy versus Practice

Managers may ask, "But, if employment is at-will, why do I have to jump through all these hoops? Why do I have to coach, counsel, and correct if employment can be terminated at the will of either party?" (see Chapter 6). The key is in considering what you must do as compared to what you should do, for any variety of reasons. And even that is difficult, since what "should" be done is often assessed in the eye of the beholder; e.g., what is best for the employer or the employee. Barring the existence of any employment contract or collective bargaining agreement to the contrary, you do not have to coach, counsel, or correct prior to termination unless you are in a state that does not recognize at-will employment, such as Montana.[2] But go back to the beginning of this chapter and you will find the answer. You help to protect yourself and your company and reap the greatest ROI on your recruitment dollars when you protect your employees. Whether you have a corrective action policy or not, and even if you have a very clear and express at-will employment policy in your employee handbook, also consider your past practice. It is likely you have given other employees opportunities to correct their behavior or performance informally, even if not formally. So, ensure your action is consistent with not just your written policy but also your past practice. Do so not because you have to do the same thing for every employee but because you need to be able to distinguish why you did "x" in one instance and "y" in another. Consider the discussion we just had under the element of lack of discrimination and equal versus equitable treatment.

Here is another common situation I have encountered. An employer has a leave of absence policy that reads that an employee may take an unpaid leave of absence not to exceed 30 days. On the 31st day of leave a manager wants to terminate an employee's employment. The HR representative, however, is aware of at least two prior instances in which "good" employees had *not* been terminated immediately after 30 days. This does not mean the manager cannot go ahead and terminate employment. It should, however, raise a flag to simply ask, "Why?" How is the current situation different from the previous situations? Is there a good business justification for treating this employee differently? For example, perhaps the two prior incidents involved long-term, high-performing employees who needed only two additional weeks of leave and it would have taken at least that long to fill their positions. The current employee may have worked for the company less than one year, has documented poor performance, and the employee's expected return to work date is "unknown." Add to these any legal considerations such as providing leave as a reasonable accommodation under the ADA (see Chapter 4).

Remember that your company's practice can be just as important as your company's policy. Also, read through your employee handbook or employment policies. Run a search for the words "will" or "shall," and where it refers to corrective action or termination, consider replacing those words with "may." Don't back yourself into a corner. If you indicate that something "will" happen, you may lose the ability to exercise management discretion, and you may lose the ability to treat employees equitably versus equally. When you indicate that something "will" happen, then you must take the defensive position of justifying why you did *not* do something. When you indicate that something "may" happen, you retain the right to determine if and when it will happen.

Adverse Impact Analysis

Do you know the demographics of your last ten involuntary terminations, or your discharges in the last six months? In the last year? If not, you should. It is a proactive practice to track and monitor at least the age, race, and sex of employees who have been involuntarily terminated from employment. Employers with 100 or more employees (and certain federal contractors) are already required to collect data on the sex and race of their employees for EEO-1 and affirmative action purposes. Employers with fewer than 100 employees and those not required to have written affirmative action plans should consult with legal counsel about collecting this data, inviting employees to self-identify using a voluntary self-identification form as there are some associated risks as well as benefits in doing so. Once collected, you can conduct a wide variety of analyses, such as the age, sex, or race of employees who are involuntarily terminated (as well as who voluntarily terminate) as compared to the same demographics of your workforce at large. For example, if 20 percent of your total workforce is age 40 or above (the ages protected against discrimination under the Age Discrimination in Employment Act, or ADEA) yet 50 percent of your involuntary terminations have been employees age 40 or above, those figures may appear to be statistically, significantly disparate. This may lead you to analyze those results and try to determine why a significantly larger percentage of your terminations are employees age 40 or above than are represented in your workforce as a whole. The same analyses may be conducted based on sex and race. Also consider whether a statistically significant number of terminations are occurring in a particular department, under a particular manager, within a particular location or business unit. Here you may see a pattern that may not necessarily give rise to a legal issue but rather to an opportunity to dialogue with that manager about his management style and expectations, and to share the objective data so that manager can consider why separations from his department are occurring at a rate higher than the company average. Being forewarned is being forearmed. You want to be aware of these trends before they are pointed out to you by an external party such as the federal Equal Employment Opportunity Commission (EEOC), state or local human relations commission, or a plaintiff's attorney.

Also, consider if there have been any unusual recent events such as a female employee informing you that she is or is trying to become pregnant; an employee requesting leave under the Family and Medical Leave Act; an employee filing a workers' compensation claim; or an employee engaging in any other legally protected activity. If the answer is "yes," this does not mean you should not proceed as planned. It will, however, enable you to review and confirm your pre-termination checklist (see Appendix).

Finally, tracking the demographics of your voluntary terminations can be valuable as well. It may be proactive to understand not just why employees are leaving your organization (addressed in exit interviews below) but who is leaving. Are there any groups that voluntarily leave your organization at a statistically significantly higher rate than other groups such as men, women, minorities, people under age 40, or people 40 or above? Exit interviews can be a great way to learn more about why people are voluntarily leaving your organization and what practices you might modify to increase retention. See Chapter 8 for more information about stay interviews and retention strategies.

Exit Interviews

Exit interviews can be a great, easy, and inexpensive way to gather data, proactively monitor the reasons your employees are leaving, and look for trends. I find most employers who conduct exit interviews do so for employees voluntarily leaving and not for employees who are involuntarily terminated. But when asked what they do with the data the answer I often hear is, "I don't know" or "nothing." The data is collected but not used in any practical way. Exit interviews can be conducted in person or electronically. Using an Excel spreadsheet, you can track the results by department, location, job classification, race, sex, age, and more. This data can be very valuable to not only signal any adverse trends — such as a statistically significant difference in the separation rate for men versus women, for persons age 40 or above, or for minorities as compared to non-minorities — but to also provide feedback to department directors and plant managers who may have a higher than average turnover rate as compared to the organization as a whole.

Consider the following:
- Do you know what your company's current turnover rate is?
- Do you know what your average cost per hire is?
- Do you know how those rates compare to the standard rate for your industry?
- Are you tracking separations by departments or locations to watch for separation rates that are higher than the company average as a whole?

- Do you know why your employees are leaving? Are the separations predominantly voluntary or involuntary?
- What are the key reasons employees are voluntarily separating? Is it for better wages, and/or benefit?

These are just a few metrics of which you may want to be aware, whether you are the HR administrator for your company or a business owner, manager, or supervisor. There are a number of resources for finding formulas and tools by which to calculate and track these metrics.[3]

Why conduct exit interviews? Every time an employee leaves it costs your company money: from advertising, to interviewing, to conducting reference and background checks, to bringing the employee on board, and providing training and education on your company's policies, procedures, and job expectations. This is another metric that you should be aware of and that is mentioned above. What is your company's cost per hire? Which recruiting sources produce the most and best hires for you? All these and more add to the learning curve during which your new employee's productivity may reasonably be below the average as they are oriented and learn your way of doing things. So, if you can retain your top performers, you can save the company money. And, if the company saves money, that leaves funds available to enhance benefits, compensation, and more.

Why else should an employer conduct exit interviews? Have you ever been surprised to look at your mail and see the return address from the EEOC or your state or local commission on human relations? Why would an employee file a charge of discrimination with a government agency without ever bringing the concern to the employer's attention first? The answer I most frequently hear is "trust" — a lack thereof. Trust is a big issue for employees. Sometimes it is a matter of believing that the company or a management representative will retaliate in some way against the employee if he complains internally. Sometimes it is a matter of believing that the employer will do nothing to rectify the situation. I find the latter even more frequently than the former. The person or practice that is frustrating the employee has gone on for a long period of time and is well known to the company, at least to several members of management, but nothing has been done to correct the matter. That is not just my experience. See Chapter 5 for more information on related research and findings from the Workplace Bullying Institute. Often the problem involves a management team member who lacks certain interpersonal skills or is perceived as being a bully. With no trust or confidence that the company will do anything about it, the employee simply resigns and/or seeks an external resource.

Ensure that your company has a policy that provides one or more resources to whom an employee can report any work-related concerns, particularly those related to actual or perceived wage disparities, discrimination, or harassment. Also ensure that it is your company's practice to promptly investigate such concerns, commit to ensuring no employee is subject to retaliation for expressing any concerns and taking immediate and appropriate remedial action (see Chapter 5).

Severance

When it comes to involuntary separation from employment, the question is sometimes asked, "Should I offer this employee a severance package?" This practice is common in the case of an individual job abolishment, individual or group layoffs, or plant closings. But what about when the job is still needed but the employee isn't? The employee has not engaged in any form of misconduct, but the employer feels the employment relationship is not salvageable. It is not a good match and the employee needs to go. A severance package is sometimes offered in this situation. It may be wise to have legal counsel draft or review any severance package you offer, particularly if you include in the package a waiver of the employee's right to sue your company. Most severance packages include such a waiver. The waiver often offers the employee salary continuation or severance pay for a certain period of time (and sometimes continued benefits such as health care coverage) in exchange for the employee waiving his right to sue the company for a wide variety of possible claims under federal, state, and local laws, as well as common law.

Another question often asked is, "If I give one person a severance package, am I obligated to do the same for every other employee I terminate?" As described earlier, this is a question of equal versus equitable treatment. An employer should consider why it is offering this benefit to one employee and not another. There can be myriad reasons that may justify this difference in treatment, such as length of service and the reason for termination.

For persons age 40 or above, the Older Workers Benefit Protection Act (OWBPA) requires that, in order for such a waiver to be valid, the waiver agreement must include the following elements[4]:

1. It must be written in a manner calculated to be understood by the individual or by the average individual eligible to participate in the severance program. Employers should take into account such factors as the level of comprehension and education of typical participants. Consideration of these factors usually will require the limitation or elimination of technical jargon and of long, complex sentences.

2. It must be in writing.

3. It must not have the effect of misleading, misinforming, or failing to inform participants and affected individuals. Any advantages or disadvantages described shall be presented without either exaggerating the benefits or minimizing the limitations.

4. It must refer to the Age Discrimination in Employment Act (ADEA) by name in connection with the waiver.

5. It must advise the employee in writing to consult an attorney before agreeing.

6. It must not require the individual to waive rights or claims that may arise after the date the waiver is executed. This does not prohibit the enforcement of agreements to perform future employment-related actions such as the employee's agreement to retire or otherwise terminate employment at a future date, so long as such agreement is not contrary to any other requirements of the ADEA.

7. It must be in exchange for consideration in addition to anything of value to which the individual already is entitled. This means the employer must provide the employee with something, such as severance pay, that is in addition to that to which the individual is already entitled in the absence of a waiver. For example, if your company has

a policy in its handbook that provides that any employee whose job is abolished will be given two weeks' pay, then the employer must give the employee with more than two weeks' pay in order for the waiver to be enforceable.

8. It must give an employee a period of at least 21 days within which to consider the agreement. An employee may sign the waiver before the 21 days has expired but must be given at least 21 days. If an employee volunteers to sign the agreement the same day he receives it, it may be a proactive practice to advise the employee to take some additional time, read the agreement thoroughly, and to consult with an attorney before signing.

9. It must also provide the individual with a period of at least seven days following the execution of such agreement (the day the individual signs it), to revoke the agreement. The agreement shall not become effective or enforceable until the revocation period has expired. Thus, it can also be a proactive practice to wait to issue the first severance payment until at least the eighth day after an employee has signed the agreement.

In the case of a group termination or exit incentive program, the same rules as described above apply to waivers in severance agreements for persons age 40 or above except that the employer must provide up to 45 days to consider the agreement. The employer must also provide each employee with additional information including but not limited to eligibility factors; time limits; job titles and ages of all employees who are eligible; and the ages of all individuals in the same job classifications or organizational unit who are not eligible.[5] This is why it is advisable to have an attorney review these agreements, whether they are for one individual or a group of individuals, to ensure that your company is complying with a number of federal, state, or local laws and regulations that dictate what these agreements must have (or not have) to be enforceable.

There is also language that may need to be added under the Defend Trade Secrets Act if the agreement includes any non-disclosure agreement (NDA) or related provisions.[6]

Unemployment Insurance

Another common question of employers (and employees) is, "Will this employee be eligible for unemployment insurance?" That answer rests with the state agency reviewing the claim. Each state has its own code for granting, denying, and administering benefits paid from the state's unemployment insurance (UI) trust fund. A good answer to give an employee may be to provide the employee with the information, such as the website to the state agency through which he can file a claim for benefits. Let the employee know that the employer does not make the final determination regarding eligibility for benefits; the state agency will determine eligibility. Although the rules vary from state to state, there are some commonalities. Generally, an employee may be eligible for UI benefits whether the employee quits or whether the employee is fired. The question in either case is "Why?" If the employee quit for "good cause" including a reason connected to the job, such as a change in wages, hours, or some condition of employment, then the employee may be eligible for benefits. An employee might also be eligible if he quit for "valid circumstance," which may include a reason not connected to the job but for a compelling personal reason, such as to care for a terminally ill family member. In this instance, the employee may be required to show that he sought an alternative, such as a flexible schedule or transfer to another position, before resigning. If the employee is fired for some level of misconduct, then the employee may be disqualified depending upon the nature of the misconduct, the employer's policies, and whether the employee received any advance notice (i.e., coaching, counseling, or corrective action) prior to the termination. Once again, you can probably see that documentation can be critical to successfully defending why an employee should or should not be eligible for benefits (see Chapter 2).

Employers pay a tax for UI benefits that, for most employers (nonprofit employers may be taxed differently), is based, in part, on the company's experience rating. The more claims that are paid to your employees, the higher your experience rating and the higher your UI tax premium may be. Documenting performance problems and talking to your employee about the need to improve, as well as setting goals and objectives, can save your company money.

If you have never been to an unemployment insurance hearing, call your HR administrator or the person who handles the company's UI claims and ask if you may attend the next hearing next time one of your employees separates from employment. The experience can be quite educational and can give you insight into how your state's agency assesses separations, what documentation they are seeking, and how you can save your company money.

Practical Tips

- Get the big picture. Even if you are sure termination is the correct next step, run it by your HR representative or legal counsel. While your plan of action may be consistent with the past practice in your department, human resources can monitor and provide you with the overall company practice to ensure consistency across the organization, watch for company-wide trends or patterns, and ensure that any termination is well-documented and based upon valid business reasons.
- Don't just open your employee handbook to be sure termination is in accordance with your policy; be sure it is also consistent with how the company has treated other employees in similar situations. If it is not, then you should have a bona fide and business-related reason for treating this employee differently.
- Consider conducting an adverse impact analysis to be sure this termination will not appear to establish a pattern or practice of treating members of any protected class (based at least on sex, race, or age) differently from other legally protected groups. If it does, be able to provide a bona fide business reason as to how and why you have arrived at your decision.
- Follow your pre-termination checklist.

2

Document, Document, Document!

How many times have you asked a manager or been asked by human resources or legal counsel for documentation when it comes to issuing corrective action or terminating an employee? Is it better to have none or some? Well, that depends upon the quality of your documentation. If your forms, notes, and performance appraisals are not accurate, then they can become weapons that can be used against you. Too often it is the case that a manager wants to terminate an employee for unsatisfactory work performance and a recent performance appraisal indicates the employee's performance meets or even exceeds expectations. Or there is at least no documentation indicating there are any performance issues. Why? Sometimes it may seem easier to soft sell a performance appraisal and avoid the time and potential conflict of setting expectations and quantifying what aspects of performance are unsatisfactory. Other times it just seems like a hassle to find the time to sit down and document an employee's unsatisfactory work performance. What you document, and where and how you document, can vary, but doing so can be critical to supporting your business justification for taking adverse employment action; e.g., firing, not promoting, or issuing corrective action to an employee. Without good documentation, it may be hard to show that your reasons were business related and not based upon the employee's membership in a protected class. Here are a few tips.

What

Hopefully you are in your particular job because you have a passion or at least a preference for what you do. Whether you own or manage an auto body shop, lawn care service, or property management firm, or are in the academic, health care/human services, technology, or any other business or industry, it is hopefully because you have a particular interest in that line of work. What you likely did not anticipate (except for those of you reading this who are HR professionals) is managing all the myriad issues that come with managing employment relationships.

The good news is that you are not expected to document every conversation that you have with every employee. You should document by exception. Document the exceptionally good and the exceptional not-so-good events, activities, and behaviors. If you go to work tomorrow and everything pretty much goes as expected, you would likely document very little or nothing with regard to employment activities. If you go to work tomorrow, however, and overhear an employee make a rude or derogatory comment, you might document that. In this case, it may not need to be formal, perhaps just a note to the file (not the HR file but to a "working file" you might maintain on your employees) or in your calendar of events. And don't forget the positive, too! When we talk about documenting performance it seems it is so often focusing on ensuring we have back-up for an upcoming, unsatisfactory performance appraisal, decision to not promote, termination, or other adverse employment action. Give the same dedication and attention to excellent performance. When you receive a customer or client compliment, jot a note, make a copy, or put a special notation in the employee's file and share it with the employee. We can all use a pat on the back every now and then.

Where

Documentation does not have to be formal. As described above, it can be a casual note that is placed in a manager's "working" file that is kept in the manager's desk and not in the employee's HR or personnel file. On the other hand, documents such as corrective or disciplinary action notices, performance appraisals, or letters of commendation are usually placed in the employee file. These become a part of the regular employment record and the employee may have access to these records, in accordance with your state law and/or company policy. Some states require that an employee be permitted access to these records at certain times and under certain circumstances. Check with your legal counsel, because how you maintain and use certain documents can determine whether they can be "discovered" in anticipation of litigation.

When

I find a common question is, "When do I move from documenting in my 'working' or informal file to issuing corrective action that will go into the employee's HR or personnel file?" Documentation should be a constant and regular practice. When you move from this type of informal documentation to the formal notice of corrective action may be dependent upon many factors, including the severity or frequency of the behavior, prior coaching or counseling, the employee's intent, and more. For example, if an employee intentionally punches a coworker, you may take formal corrective action immediately such as suspending the employee pending the outcome of your investigation. On the other hand, if an employee is late one or two mornings, you may be more likely to mention it to the employee but wait until a third, or fourth lateness in a particular period of time before issuing any formal corrective action. If two employees make the same procedural error, you might also decide to issue corrective action to one and not the other because you have already coached the former on the procedure on one or two prior occasions and this is the latter employee's first procedural error. Each instance should be assessed on a case-by-case basis to determine the most appropriate action.

The performance appraisal is an area that frequently lacks consistency. Many companies have a policy that reads that performance appraisals (or evaluations or reviews) will be conducted annually. Be sure that is defined. Does that mean the appraisal will be conducted on or about the same date every year for all employees, such as January 1? Or does that mean appraisals will be conducted on each employee's anniversary date determined by the employee's date of hire? If the employee transfers to another job or is promoted or demoted, does that establish a new anniversary date? You may set any date you like. Once that date is set, however, be sure the appraisals are completed in a timely fashion, particularly if your policy reads that they "will" happen rather than they "generally will" or "may" happen annually. Delaying or skipping appraisals may give the appearance of adverse treatment if one employee has not had an evaluation in the last two years while others have regularly received annual performance appraisals. Or imagine you want to issue corrective action or terminate employment of the employee described above because his performance is now unsatisfactory. If the employee was not given an appraisal and feedback that could have been helpful in enhancing his performance, the question may be raised as to why you violated your own policy in not issuing a timely performance appraisal. That question can be exacerbated if the employee in question claims a difference in treatment based on his membership in a protected class.

How

Objective rather than subjective documentation is another key. Let's say you have an administrative assistant who is making many errors. Telephone numbers in messages are transposed, records are misfiled, and typed memos are fraught with typographical or grammatical errors. An example of subjective documentation might be to write, "Your error rate is too high." Does that statement set the expectation? Does it tell the employee what the error rate should be? Where it is now? What is too high? You should also ensure the error rate is higher than the error rate of other employees in the same job classification or same department who have not received comparable coaching or counseling.

What is the standard or acceptable error rate? Objective documentation quantifies the behavior being described. An example of objective documentation might be to write, "You are averaging 40 words per minute while the departmental average for administrative assistants is 55 words per minute." The same challenges and examples are often found when reviewing documentation related to attendance and punctuality. An employee is described as being "excessively" late or absent. But the reader has no idea what that means. Is the employee late an average of once per week or per month? Quantify, quantify, quantify. Soft skills like providing quality customer service can be a bit more difficult to quantify but you can attach measurable standards to them as well. How do you objectively document an employee's poor customer service skills? Perhaps you measure customer service by the number of customer complaints. So instead of telling an employee, "You need to improve your customer service skills," which is subjective and for which the employee may have no idea what you expect, you might say, "I expect to receive zero complaints regarding your customer service skills over the next 30 days."

Also be sure that you have communicated the expectation to the employee in advance. Do not wait until the employee has failed to meet your expectations to then tell the employee what that expectation is. Be proactive. Make it a part of your departmental orientation process to tell employees your departmental as well as job-specific expectations (see Chapter 8). A departmental orientation could include not just an orientation to the employee's particular job and related duties but to your departmental expectations including but not limited to things like dress code, telephone use, attendance, and punctuality standards.

Why

Sometimes we wonder, "Why do I have to go through all this? Shouldn't an employee know what kind of attire is unprofessional and that he should come to work every day and on time?" While some may think the answer is "Yes," work environments vary much more today than they did 20 years ago. Dress codes, for example, range from professional to business casual to casual, and how employers define each of those also varies. The definition of proper workplace attire can vary dramatically from industry to industry, as well as between companies within the same industry. With the advent of flexible work schedules and work locations including telecommuting, the lines have blurred with regard to "attending" work in the office as compared to attending from home. Even methods of communicating have varied. I had a conversation with a manager who was frustrated because she felt the employee was not only absent and late frequently but the employee would send a text message to the manager instead of calling the manager by telephone directly. I understood *what* was frustrating her so we talked about *why* that frustrated her. The manager felt texting was disrespectful; she wanted to be called by telephone. We then focused on the business need that was not being met. The manager admitted the texts were timely and in advance of any absence or lateness. So there was no adverse impact to business operations by receiving a text instead of a phone call. It was just this manager's personal preference to receive a phone call. We then went to our elements of just cause and found our answer in the first one: forewarning. The manager acknowledged that she had never set an express expectation that employees notify her of an absence or lateness by telephone rather than by text. The manager acknowledged that text messaging may seem quite acceptable to some but it was not to her. Lesson learned? Don't assume, be clear, and let your employees know in advance what is expected of them.

Making the Most of Performance Appraisals

There are a variety of terms used for the strategies employers use to provide feedback to employees regarding their performance. The term "performance appraisal" is often used interchangeably with "performance evaluation" and "performance review." For our purposes, we will consider these terms to refer to the same process: a periodic assessment of one or more aspects of an employee's work performance that is documented in writing, by one or more persons, including the employee's immediate supervisor, and is shared with the employee orally or in writing.

Performance Management versus Performance Development

These terms are broader than performance appraisal. Performance management may refer to a broad, umbrella term used to describe an entire array of activities in which an employer may engage to maintain employees' work performance at a desire level and quality. This may include orientation, coaching, counseling, correcting, appraising, training, and more.

Performance development is one aspect of performance management by which the employer may provide sources for growing, advancing, and/or enhancing individual or team knowledge, skills, or abilities. This is often a part of succession planning, mentoring, and job shadowing programs.

For purposes of this book, we will consider performance appraisals to be tools by which an employer attempts to manage rather than develop employee performance.

To Pay or Not to Pay — For Performance

Extensive research has been conducted to assess the pros and cons of associating pay with performance. I find the results mixed. But more recently with increasing frequency I find research and studies finding more problems than benefits.

Some suggest incentive based pay can be detrimental.[1] Some suggest doing away with performance appraisals altogether.[2] Some suggest the results are not reaping the benefits sought or the programs are not really tied to performance although they may be tagged with the name "merit"- or "performance"-based pay. For example, a survey conducted by Willis Towers Watson found among other things that only 20 percent of survey respondents found merit pay to be effective at driving higher levels of individual performance at their organization and 71 percent use local market data to establish their merit-based budget, a practice that looks more like a cost-of-living adjustment (COLA).[3] SHRM has gathered a variety of articles, resources, and tools employers may consider before implementing a new or modifying an existing process.[4] If you decide to implement a new or update an existing performance appraisal or review process the following are some components to take into consideration.

Who

There is a wide variety of performance appraisal processes from which to choose. Who participates is just one factor that varies among some of these. There are at least two components to this question: Who will participate as a rater, appraiser, or evaluator, and who will participate as the person being rated? Let us consider the former first.

Most everyone is familiar with the traditional appraisal process by which an employee's manager or supervisor gives the employee a written performance appraisal. In this process the employee tends to be fairly passive, receiving the feedback, commenting, but usually without any formal documentation being required as a part of the process.

The next step may be to add a self-appraisal component. This often provides the employee with a form (hard copy or electronic) that is nearly identical to the form the manager completes and by which the employee can appraise his own performance using the same factors and the same rating scale as the manager. The two then meet, compare their responses, and hopefully engage in an interactive dialogue comparing and contrasting their respective responses. The manager retains the final say as to what actual ratings the employee receives but the self-appraisal can become a part of the official record and may be placed in the employee's HR file along with the manager's appraisal of the employee. This process more actively engages the employee and can help the manager better understand the employee's perception of the employee's own performance.

Peer reviews may be used less frequently. When they are used, I find more often than not that they are used in particular industries such as health care or human services or firms that regularly work in a collaborative environment like those in the design and marketing fields. In this process, not only does the employee's manager complete an appraisal of the employee's performance but so do some or all of the employee's peers, colleagues, or team members. The results may be shared in a peer review meeting, or individual results may be compiled into an average composite and shared with the employee in a one-on-one meeting with the employee's manager.

The most inclusive process may be the 360-degree appraisal process by which the employee's performance is appraised by the employee, the manager, the employee's peers, and the employee's direct reports (if any). Sometimes clients or customers are included in this process as well. The results are generally computerized or compiled into a composite result that compares overall ratings from each group with the overall ratings of the other groups. This gives the employee insight as to how his self-perception of his performance compares to that of his manager, peers, direct reports, and/or clients and customers. More often than not, this process is not tied to compensation but is used as a performance development tool.

But who in your organization will be appraised using your company's tool and process? Everyone? Staff only? Staff and managers? Executives? And how will the results be practically used? For example, how do you ensure managers attached the same meaning to each of the ratings available to them? (See the discussion of ratings in "How" below). Calibration is a process by which the organization engages at least some portion of its workforce in interactive discussions to ensure consistency in the meaning of performance ratings. For example, when two managers from different departments rate two different employees a "4 – Above Average" on a particular duty or responsibility they mean the same thing and the respective performance levels are comparable.[5] In a 2013 Global Performance Management Assessment Survey published by Mercer, 54 percent of the respondents indicated they use calibration with all employees; 11 percent use it with managers and above; 10 percent with executives only; 6 percent with directors and above; and 20 percent did not use calibration.[6] So it seems, like so many HR and employment practices, there is no "right" answer. Work backwards (like this book). Ask yourself what *your* company's goals are in using the performance appraisal process; why are you doing it? The answer to that question will likely be a good first step in determining who should or should not be included in the process.

What

What factors or behaviors should be appraised or evaluated? The answer to this question may again be best provided by the organization. Getting feedback from focus groups that include executive team members, middle and front-line managers, as well as staff, is one strategy. This can be proactive and helpful in capturing the common and key factors and behaviors that your organization thinks are critical to successful performance, both individual and operational. For example, in a marketing firm, creativity may be highly valued and an important component of every employee's job as the business strives to create new and appealing ads for its clients. In manufacturing, however, where quality control requires zero deviation by employees working on the assembly line, creativity may not be desired and might actually be a hindrance to satisfactory work performance.

Another strategy is to develop a performance appraisal template. The core template can include sections for behaviors common to and expected of all employees, such as attendance, punctuality, work performance (what you do), and conduct (how you go about doing it). Depending upon the industry, you might add a section for safety as well. But the section related to work performance, which includes the employee's duties and responsibilities, may be different for each job title and mirrors the essential functions for any particular job.

No matter what strategy you use, it will be important to focus on what is important to your company's successful performance and develop corresponding behavioral and objective measures for that performance. For example, rather than rating an administrative assistant as to how well the employee "Completes projects in a timely manner," rate the employee using objective measures such as "Completes projects as scheduled at least 90 percent of the time." Another option is to keep the question as is and use a rating scale that quantifies the performance. See the next section on "How" for an example.

Finally, you can develop the very best tool, but if there is no account-ability built into your process, it is less likely to succeed. Are your managers held accountable for not just completing performance appraisals for each of their employees but for completing them in a timely manner? If so, how? You could do so, for example, by including timely completion of performance appraisals as a behavior to be rated on each appraisal form that is to be used to appraise managers' performance. Example: "Completes 100 percent of the assigned performance appraisals in a timely manner (within 30 days of the due date) in the last year."

How

I have mentioned "rating" several times throughout this section. But what does that mean? Performance can be appraised using a numerical scale, narrative format, or a combination of the two. The latter seems to be a common market practice. Managers may rate employee performance on a scale of 1 to 4, 1 to 5, or some other range. But which scale should you use and what does each represent? Even-numbered scales, like 1 to 4 or 1 to 10, are forced-choice scales; the rater is forced to rate the individual slightly above or slightly below the mid-point or "average." There is no middle-of-the-road. Some prefer this scale because it avoids the error of central tendency (read on; it's coming up under the section on Rating Errors and Rating Biases). Others dislike it because it cannot accurately reflect the performance of an employee who is truly performing at just a satisfactory level and meeting expectations. Thus, the latter may prefer to use an odd-numbered scale such as 1 to 5 that does provide a mid-point and reflects performance that is satisfactory and meets all expectations, not slightly above or below that middle level. Opponents of this methodology are concerned this may lead to the error of central tendency in which the manager might take the easy route and just mark everyone right down the middle of the scale, giving little thought to the process.

Once you have selected the areas of performance to be appraised (what) and the scale to be used (how), you might next consider whether or not the performance areas will be weighted equally. For example, let's say you rate performance in the four areas:

1. Attendance/punctuality.
2. Conduct/attitude.
3. Performance of job duties.
4. Safety.

A manufacturing company might weight safety slightly higher than conduct/attitude so that it accounts for 30 percent of an employee's overall rating, conduct/attitude account for 20 percent, and the other two areas account for 25 percent each.

As for including a narrative portion of feedback exclusively or in combination with a numerical scale, ensure participants, particularly managers are trained in writing objectively rather than subjectively. As described earlier in this chapter, for example, if a manager writes, "Christine's productivity is below average," do we really know at what level the employee is performing or where she should be? And based on what average, departmental? By job?

Organizationally? A clearer appraisal might read, "Christine's average weekly productivity is 100 calls per week; that is the lowest in the department and 20 percent below the departmental average of 125 calls per week." Also consider including as a part of your performance appraisal process a step that includes an opportunity for review, such as by human resources, before the final appraisal is placed in the employee's file. This can provide one more perspective to help ensure goals and comments are written objectively and rating errors or rating biases are avoided.

Types of Appraisals

Before implementing or updating your appraisal process, research it. See what others in your industry are doing.

360/Multi-Rater

This involves a process by which information is collected from the employee's supervisor, colleagues, and subordinates about an individual's work-related behavior and its impact. Other names for this approach include multi-rater feedback, multi-source feedback, or group review. This form of appraisal is widely favored for employee development purposes.

Behaviorally Anchored Rating Systems

The behaviorally anchored rating systems (BARS) process attempts to assess employee behavior rather than specific characteristics. The appraisal tool generally contains a set of specific behaviors that represent gradations of performance and are used as common reference points, called "anchors," for rating employees on various job dimensions. Developing a BARS assessment tool is time-consuming and can be expensive because it is based on extensive job analysis and the collection of critical incidents for each specific job.

Competency-Based

This type of a system focuses on performance as measured against specified competencies (knowledge, skills, and abilities or KSAs) as opposed to specific tasks or behaviors that are identified for each position.

Forced Distribution

In this process the ratings of employees in a particular group are disbursed along a bell-shaped curve, with the supervisor allocating a certain percentage of the ratings within the group to each performance level on the scale. The actual distribution of employee performance may not actually resemble a bell curve, so supervisors may be forced to include some employees at either end of the scale when they would otherwise place them somewhere in the middle.

Graphic Rating Scales

Because of its simplicity, graphic rating scales (GRS) tends to be one of the most frequently used forms of performance appraisal. These appraisals list a number of factors, including general behaviors and characteristics (e.g., attendance, dependability, quality of work, quantity of work, and relationships with people) on which a supervisor rates an employee. The rating is usually based on a scale of three to five gradations (e.g., unsatisfactory, marginal, satisfactory, highly satisfactory, and outstanding). This type of system allows the rater to determine the performance of an employee along a continuum.

Management by Objectives

Management by objectives (MBO) is a process through which goals are set collaboratively for the organization as a whole, various departments, and each individual member. Employees are evaluated annually based on how well they have achieved the results specified by the goals. MBO is particularly applicable to non-routine jobs, such as those of managers, project leaders, and individual contributors.

Peer Review

This process is less comprehensive than but similar to the 360 assessment process. It involves collecting information from the employee's peers only about an individual's work-related behavior and its impact. Like the 360, this form of appraisal may be used for employee development purposes.

Ranking

This process consists of listing all employees in a designated group from highest to lowest in order of performance. The primary drawback is that quantifying the differences in individual performance is difficult and may involve drawing very narrow — if not meaningless — distinctions. It may also skew results where an entire team is low-performing but, by definition, must rank someone as a top performer of the group.

There are many options, and learning more about each will help you make the best decision as to the right "fit" for your organization.

A final note on "how" would be about training. So often employees or managers are given a blank appraisal form and told to complete it. It seems pretty straightforward, right? You will recall that I mentioned using feedback from focus groups to develop your appraisal tool, including feedback from staff. You may find there are many components of the performance appraisal process of which your staff and managers are not aware or do not understand: "How does the appraisal affect my pay?" "What if I don't agree, can I put something in my HR file?" "What if I don't get my annual appraisal?" "What if my employee won't complete the self-appraisal form?"

One of my (several) memorable lessons from when I was in HR administration was with an employee who had received her first performance appraisal at the end of her introductory period). She received a low rating for attendance and punctuality. One of her complaints was, "If I had known attendance and punctuality were weighted so heavily I wouldn't have been late so much!" While that recollection makes me smile to this day, and I still think it was not a very good excuse for excessive lateness, it was a teachable moment for us as the employer. We failed to set the expectation for that employee from day one. (Of course now I must refer you to Chapter 3.) From that point on we included a blank copy of our performance appraisal in the new hire packet and incorporated a brief overview of the performance appraisal process in our new employee orientation program (see Chapter 8).

And don't forget your managers. Train them with the same core information you provide to employees. Help prepare them for likely employee responses, such as managing emotional reactions (see Chapter 3); what your company's process is for rebuttals (*can* an employee put a written response in his HR file or file a grievance?); information on common rating errors and biases so they can avoid them by being aware of them (see next section); and more.

Rating Errors and Rating Biases

Search the employment headlines and it is not hard to find a reference to performance appraisals being used by the plaintiff as evidence of discrimination. Not because the employee received a poor rating, just the opposite. The employee received an exemplary rating and shortly thereafter was terminated for unsatisfactory work performance.

All too often, it may seem easier to go ahead and give an employee a satisfactory rating on a performance appraisal rather than managing the potential conflict and emotional reactions that can come with telling an employee that his performance is not meeting expectations. Instead, be candid, and be objective. The following are some common rating errors or biases that you should keep in mind and avoid when completing performance appraisals.

Halo Effect

This results when we unintentionally permit an employee's competency in one area to overshadow incompetency in other areas. I see this happen more often than not in technical or sales positions. You may have heard of the "Peter Principle" developed by Dr. Laurence J. Peter and Raymond Hull in their classic book, *The Peter Principle*, which maintains that employees tend to rise to their level of incompetence.[7] How? Employers promote them to that level. Why? Sometimes we want to reward a top performer, such as an employee who is technically savvy or makes a lot of sales or brings in lots of new clients. So we promote the person to a team leader, supervisor, manager, and/or director. In that process we may not have given sufficient thought to the person's management skills (or lack thereof). Next thing you know, the person is no longer performing any of the technical, sales or business development work at which he was so good. Now he is managing people with no clue as to how to do so efficiently.

Horns Effect

This is essentially the opposite of the halo effect. When an employee is particularly poorly skilled in one area and we let that overshadow his competencies in other areas. It may also describe a manager who has a personal dislike or animus against an employee, thus the manager is the one wearing the horns and gives the employee inaccurate and poor performance ratings based on his personal dislike rather than realistic appraisal of the employee's performance.

Primacy Effect

This is the tendency to let the first impression overshadow other, subsequent behavior. Have you ever had a star employee and then wondered what happened the day after the introductory or probationary period was over? The person shined and then as soon as he felt he was "in" the sheen began to dull. Sometimes we become so enamored with our new star employee that we fail to see the slow decline in performance and continue to see the employee as he was in that honeymoon stage of the employment relationship. You can avoid this by making periodic reviews of work performance and focusing on quality, quantity, attendance, punctuality, etc. Checking these for all your employees on at least a quarterly basis can help you proactively monitor performance and prevent the company and coworkers from being burdened with an individual who is no longer carrying his share of the workload.

Error of Central Tendency

This occurs when we rate all employees within a narrow range regardless of differences in individual performance. This may be the result of an attempt to avoid conflict. Rather than taking the time to distinguish the high from the low performers a manager may simply rate all employees as satisfactory. It may be faster and easier in the short run but not when you need an accurate performance appraisal to substantiate your need to terminate an employee for poor performance; having an unrealistic, satisfactory appraisal can work against you. This rating error more frequently occurs when using odd-numbered rating scales such as 1 to 5.

Recency Effect

Opposite of the primacy effect, this is the tendency to let the last event overshadow prior behaviors. Sometimes this is the case when a very recent event, positive or negative, has occurred and is overshadowing your recollection of the employee's prior performance. Something recently went very awry and is wiping out your recollection of all the good work the employee has done over the last year. Or the employee just did a great job such as inventing a new process that will reduce costs and generate revenue for the company and you are discounting his lack of performance over the last year. Again, this is where your informal documentation can help you recall the quality of work and related issues that have arisen over time.

Leniency Error

This error occurs when we rate all employees favorably to avoid giving low marks. This error may have the greatest potential to fiscally impact your budget. This may happen, not so much to avoid conflict, but when a manager feels everyone is trying to do his best despite the fact that productivity, quality, or other factors are not being met. When creating your labor budget for the upcoming fiscal year, you generally project wage increases, if any, assuming a bell shaped curve. For example, a company offers something other than a COLA such as some type of merit pay or pay for performance increase. When projecting increases for next year's budget, they may assume that most employees will fall into the middle with some outliers falling at the far ends of the performance spectrum with some high and some low performers. When this error is applied across several departments and wage increases are tied to performance evaluation ratings, it unexpectedly skews the results to the right of that bell-shaped curve, costing your company more money than budgeted because higher ratings equal higher pay increases. Remember that performance appraisals are (or should be) tied to the job duties and responsibilities, not the person. If someone is trying his best but still cannot meet job expectations, then they are not satisfactorily fulfilling the responsibilities of that job. Perhaps the selection was not a good match; e.g., it was a poor hire or the employee has not been provided with adequate training. Whatever the case, you must be candid in your assessment and determine what you can provide that employee, if anything, to enable him to meet those expectations. When intentionally applied, this is sometimes referred to as the sunflower effect: an attempt to make oneself look better as a manager by having a group of star employees.

Similar-to-Me Error

This is similar to, but different from, the sunflower effect. It may be a subconscious bias to rate an employee that we perceive to be like us (assuming we like ourselves) higher than accurately reflects the employee's performance.

When

Like so many factors in this process, it is up to you to decide when and how frequently your company will conduct performance appraisals. A common practice is annually upon each employee's anniversary date. Employers that have an introductory period often conduct a performance evaluation at the end of that period as well. As I mentioned earlier, be sure you define the term "annually" so employees know what to expect and when. Do you mean appraisals will be conducted on a calendar year basis, fiscal year basis, or on the employee's anniversary date? Smaller organizations may choose to appraise all employees at the same time and use the start or end of the calendar or fiscal year. As companies grow in size, this may become burdensome as they would have to appraise hundreds of employees at the same time. Instead, they may choose to use employees' anniversary dates. Whatever date(s) you choose, ensure they are completed in a timely manner, and define "timely" so your managers know what is expected of them as well. As mentioned at the start of this chapter, not only do inaccurate performance appraisals have the potential to create legal turmoil but the absence of an appraisal for one employee when others have received theirs may also give the appearance of adverse treatment.

Practical Tips

My father often said to me, "Do it right or don't do it at all." That lesson has served me well over the years. The thought is the same in the common phrase, "A job worth doing is worth doing well." This is probably the third time I have alluded to this concept in this chapter, but it is very important;

if you have a performance appraisal program, process, and/or policy, then be sure to follow it. Don't spend the time and energy in forming focus groups; developing tools, systems and processes; running pilot programs; and more if you are not going to hold employees and managers accountable for actively participating in the process.

- Think about when you first set your expectation. Is it on the first day of employment? That's a good start. Consider setting it even sooner. Start in the interview. See the section on Coaching in the next chapter, Chapter 3. Until then, at least set the expectation from day one; consider including a blank appraisal form in your new hire packet so employees can see, in advance, how and on what their performance will be appraised.

- Incorporate a quick review of the appraisal form and process into your new employee orientation program or onboarding process (see Chapter 8). Provide training for your staff and managers to anticipate their questions, and provide answers and practical tips for making the process easier.

- Anticipate challenges: Consider whether or not you want to include a signature line at the end of the appraisal form for the employee to sign. If so, how will you handle an employee who declines to sign? Consider including a statement that indicates that the employee's signature displays that he has received the appraisal and does not necessarily indicate that he agrees with the appraisal.

- Here's a tip from when I was in human resources: We had approximately 3,500 employees, and keeping up with the ever-changing job descriptions was becoming overwhelming for the HR staff and our management team members. To help us all stay on track, we added a question on the employees' self-appraisal form to the effect, "Does your current job description fairly and accurately describe your current duties and responsibilities? Yes/ No." If the employee checked "No," that was a flag for human resources when we received the final copy of the completed appraisal to contact the employee's manager, get his feedback, and discuss the need for a desk audit or informal review to update the job description along with the employee's input.

If you don't use self-appraisals, you can incorporate a similar structure into the traditional appraisal process with a couple of yes/no questions:

1. Did you review the employee's current job description with him?
2. Does the employee feel it fairly accurately reflects his or her current job duties? For this question, be sure to define "fairly accurately" such as, "at least 80 percent of current, primary duties and responsibilities are listed."

3

Coaching, Counseling, and Correcting

Writer and psychiatrist Theodore Rubin said, "The problem is not that there are problems. The problem is expecting otherwise and thinking that having problems is a problem."[1]

Whether your role is as an HR administrator, business owner, manager, or supervisor, you are also the complaint department. Your job is to take employees' complaints. And you know what? You should be thankful for nearly every complaint you receive. Why? It takes trust. Employees generally will not complain to someone they do not trust. So the next time an employee comes to you with a complaint, smile. Be thankful that they are complaining to you and not an external agency or opposing legal counsel. Take it as a compliment; you are trusted.

In Chapter 1 we have already mentioned employment at-will and its exceptions and we will touch on it again in Chapter 6. So here, let's just ask, "If employment is at-will, why bother with coaching, counseling, and/or correcting? Why can't I just let an employee go?" Well, generally you can), assuming your reason for terminating the employee does not establish some form of unlawful discrimination or retaliation, or have some other unlawful basis. So if it's not unlawful why *should* you coach, counsel, or correct prior to termination? That takes a lot of time and energy. But consider this. How much time, money, and energy have you already spent just bringing this person on board? Add up your advertising dollars, lower productivity during the learning curve, plus your time in recruiting, interviewing, selecting, and hiring — you have made a substantial investment in this individual. Do you really want to toss that aside and start all over again? See again some of the HR metrics mentioned in Chapter 1.

So, if we agree that there is a valid return on investment (ROI) in coaching, counseling, and correcting, then let's begin.

Coaching

What nouns and adjectives come to mind when you think of a coach? Trainer, teacher, instructor, mentor, and more? At what point do you begin setting expectations for your new employees? The first day of employment? During new employee orientation? How about during the employment interview? What better time to let a prospective employee know what you expect in your department, not to mention the organization as a whole? What is your expectation with regard to professional attire? Attendance and punctuality? Customer service?

And once the employee is on-board (see Chapter 8), how do you practically set expectations? Be specific: "I expect employees in my department to be punctual, and we do not tolerate excessive absenteeism." Does the employee know what you really expect? How is punctuality defined? Some people would say one minute late is late. On the other end of the spectrum some employers address performance without regard to *when* the work is done, offering unlimited leave and no defined work hours. The question is how do *you* define excessive absenteeism for your employees in your department? Does the reason for the absence make a difference? What if it was scheduled in advance, would that count in your definition of excessive? And how and when do you effectively communicate those expectations to your employees? Don't assume. While you know what you expect and mean, you cannot assume that the employee does. Be clear and specific: "I expect employees in my department to have no more than one unscheduled lateness and no more than one unscheduled absence each month."

Many times employees become frustrated because they thought they followed a supervisor's instruction only to learn that they had not. Clear communication of expectations is a shared responsibility. You cannot assume an employee knows what you mean when you use certain action verbs like increase, decrease, improve. Quantify, quantify, quantify. And use time tables to set your expectations. I suspect most every person reading this book has heard the acronym for giving "SMART" instructions or directions. You may have heard it before but I believe it is worth repeating and giving due consideration with practical examples. I must say before proceeding, I have found no less than eight variations of the acronym[2] and I suspect there are more. Most variations, however, focus on similar principles.

Specific

When you give an employee an instruction, be sure it is specific, such as including behavioral examples. Rather than telling an employee, "You are expected to always provide quality customer service" you might say, "You are expected to greet every customer with 'Good morning' or 'Good afternoon' and ask, 'How may I help you?' "

Measurable

Where possible, use behavioral objectives that can be measured. Rather than telling an employee, "You are expected to maintain consistently high quality with a low error rate," you might say, "You are expected to maintain consistently high quality by producing an average error rate of no more than 2 percent." As mentioned in the previous chapter, I find one of the most challenging aspects of this element arises when dealing with soft skills, such as described above; how do you measure quality customer service? Even that can be quantified by telling an employee, "We expect no customer service representative to receive more than one customer complaint per quarter."

Attainable or **A**chievable

An employee cannot succeed in performing your assigned task if he does not have the requisite knowledge, skills, and abilities (KSAs) to accomplish the task. Be sure your employee has been trained in how to do a task before expecting him to perform it. I remember a time when I was in human resources in a hospital and an employee who worked in the operating room was written up for violating the department's sterile protocol. Without going into all the detail, in short, he had not laid out the instruments the way the surgeon and department expected and had inadvertently contaminated the sterile field. His explanation was that he laid out the instruments as he was taught in medical school. Further research revealed that there were, in fact, different approaches as to how a sterile field could be established. What a teachable moment. The department needed to ensure they taught employees as to the protocol they wanted employees to follow rather than assuming that everyone followed the same protocol.

*R*ealistic, *R*esults-Oriented or *R*elevant

I distinguish this factor from the one above as extrinsic versus intrinsic. An employee may have the intrinsic or internal KSAs to get the job done but may be constrained by extrinsic factors such as not having the authority to get the job done; thus it is not realistic for the employee to be able to accomplish what you ask. Take the example of an inventory supply clerk who lets inventory levels fall below par. The employee's explanation is that he did know how, when, and from whom to order the supplies. He could not do so, however, because he was authorized to order only up to $200 of inventory. The needed supplies cost $500, and the purchasing agent who could authorize this order was on vacation. This employee was not given the resource, nor was he empowered with the authority he needed to get the job done. Yes, there is still accountability on the employee's part for not taking this a step further and asking his supervisor for assistance, but this problem was created as a result of a shared responsibility on the employer's part as well.

The task must be results-oriented to drive business results. Ensure that the employee understands not just what task is to be performed but what result or outcome is to be achieved. So like the above example, the task is maintaining sufficient inventory *and* projecting into the future to anticipate when new orders need to be placed to avoid shortages.

Similarly, the task must be relevant. This goes to *why* I have to do *what* I have to do. We will visit this in more detail below.

*T*imely

This is a common pitfall that I see frustrate employees time and time again. A manager gives an employee a task to complete "right away" or "immediately" but fails to define what that means. So when the manager subsequently asks the employee one hour later why the task has not been completed the employee replies in frustration and angst, "Really?! I didn't know you wanted me to drop everything and get it done within the hour!" Be sure to tell your employee when you want a task completed. If you are going to check in with the employee periodically, let the employee know that too and when that might occur. Employees may feel micromanaged if they are given an assignment with a 30-day window, for example and the manager checks in every week asking, "How is it coming along?" While the manager may be well-intentioned and feel he is being supportive, the employee may feel the manager does not trust him. You have likely heard about helicopter parents. Have you heard about seagull managers? The term is reported to have first been referenced in Ken Blanchard's 1985 book *Leadership and the One Minute Manager*: "Seagull managers fly in, make a lot of noise, dump on everyone, and then fly out."[3] Fast-forward to 2016 and *Forbes*[4], and *CEO*[5] magazines and many more publications all have articles about the woes that befall the workforce operating under this management style. Don't be one and don't be perceived as one. Tell your employee, in advance, not only when the task should be completed but that you may check in on him on a weekly basis in the interim. That way the expectation is set and no one should be surprised or frustrated by periodic checks.

Counseling

Now that you have set objective and measurable expectations, what if the employee is not meeting them? How can you best redirect behavior? Once again, focus on measurable performance standards. In addition, use the following tips to help the employee understand the importance of the task and the result if outcomes are not achieved.

Manage the "What" versus the "How"

Your job is to tell employees what to do; you direct, supervise, instruct, train, staff, schedule, and more. You are responsible for overseeing what employees do. However, you may not have to so closely manage *how* they do it. Of course the how is critical in certain tasks, jobs, and industries.

How a nurse pushes a syringe into a patient to administer medication is critical, but whether an administrative assistant produces a financial report in Access or Excel may not be critical so long as the data that is needed is provided. Let go! Empower your employees. I see and read so much more now on employee engagement than I do empowerment. Remember the old classics like, *Zapp! The Lightning of Empowerment*,[6] or *Who Moved My Cheese?*[7] Yet it seems to be that the two are irrevocably tied together. I cannot imagine how I can have an actively engaged employee who is not simultaneously empowered. And if I cannot have the former without the latter then empowerment must come first, a condition precedent to engagement. Think about your own personal experiences as a consumer. Have you ever been frustrated as a customer when the clerk waiting on you does not have the authority to do what you ask and it seems like such a simple thing? You want to return an item you purchased, perhaps. You don't want your money back; you only want to exchange the product for another one of a different color. The clerk tells you he is not authorized to make exchanges — only the manager can do that. So you have to stand around and wait 10 minutes until the manager finishes with another customer. Then you find all the manager does is walk over to you, ask what you want, and hand you the item of your choice. A 60-second transaction took you 10 minutes to complete because the clerk was not empowered to do this for you. Everybody loses. You lost time, the clerk lost the ability to help you and certainly did not feel empowered in having to direct you to the manager, and the store may have lost you as a customer. What about the manager? I hope his time could have been better spent performing a management-level task that simply handing me a different item. Lesson learned? Do not micro-manage your employees. Empower them as much as possible. Let go and find the freedom you will both enjoy!

Ask "How" Before "Who"

When something goes wrong, what is the first question we often ask? "Who did it?" is often the first question we ask. While that is an important question, consider making it the second question you ask. Consider making your first question, "How did that happen?" Are there certain protocols, checks, and balances that are not in place that should be? Then ask, "Who?" as an important second question to ensure the employee(s) involved has the required knowledge, skills, and abilities to perform the assigned tasks.

"I" versus "You" Statements

How often do we tell others what they have (have not) done without really knowing the facts? Have you ever called a customer service department and been told, "You dialed the wrong number." Then, when you repeat the number you dialed, the person on the other end of the line tells you, "Oh, that's this number; I guess they transferred their extension over here." "Aha!," you think. So I *did* dial the correct number. Then why did you tell me I was wrong? Or how about e-mail or voice mail? Has anyone ever told you, "Hey, you never answered my e-mail message" or "Hey, you never called me back after I left you a voice mail message."? When, in fact, you did reply but their inbox was full and would not accept any more messages? From these day-to-day experiences of people incorrectly telling us what we did or did not do we learn that it may be better to use "I" rather than "you." The same applies to managing your employees. Rather than telling your employee what he did or did not do, tell the employee what you do or do not have. For example, "I don't have the report from you that I requested to have by close of business yesterday." This gives the employee the opportunity to tell you what he did or did not do without getting frustrated because you have made an inappropriate assumption. For example, he might tell you that he put the report in your inbox at 3:00 p.m. yesterday and there is now so much stuff on top of it that you did not see it.

Why You Do What You Do

Have you ever been frustrated and wondered why an employee was not getting it? Maybe you have talked to the employee once, twice, and maybe even a third time about the same performance problem. Ask yourself this: Having told the employee what (and what not) to do, when was the last time you told the employee why it needs to be done or why it is important?

Adult learning theory contends, among many things, that adult learners seek to understand why.[8] It is not enough for us to just know what to do, we seek to understand why it should be done. Empowered employees more often than not understand how what they do contributes to the operations of the business, its mission, and more because they have been told why they do what they do. For example, a pharmacy aide is repeatedly told that he must get certain medications into the medication cart no later than 8:00 a.m. Invariably, he repeatedly gets the medications into the cart between 8:10 and 8:15. The employee is frustrated and thinks his boss is a pain and a control freak. What's the big deal? It's just 5 or 10 minutes! What the manager has never told the employee are the implications of those few minutes. What the employee does not know is that the medications are used in surgery and are picked up every 30 minutes at five and 35 minutes after the hour. So when this employee delivers the medications at 10 or 15 minutes after the hour, they will not be picked up for another 20 to 25 minutes and surgery may have to be delayed. This can have a critical and adverse outcome for the patient awaiting that surgery. If the pharmacy aide had known the implications of his actions, he might have taken greater care to be timely. But his manager never told him why, just what.

Speak Up!

How about this scenario: Have you ever been so frustrated with an employee's unsatisfactory performance that instead of giving him more work or new assignments you have just done the work yourself or reassigned it to a coworker? If you do that and say nothing to the employee, how will he learn? How will he know that his performance is unsatisfactory? Your silence may reasonably be interpreted as condoning the unsatisfactory conduct. Not to mention the frustration that a coworker may feel at having to do another employee's work. Remember the 80-20 rule or the Pareto Principle?[9] It has many applications and basically holds that 80 percent of the effects or results come from 20 percent of the causes. Applied to the workplace, examples include from the half-empty perspective that you spend 80 percent of your time on 20 percent of your employees (the problem employees whom I'll call stinkers) and from the half-full perspective,

20 percent of your employees complete 80 percent of the work (your star performers). Here you may be fostering the latter rule. Why? You have designed it that way by redistributing work assignments. You have taken the work away from your stinkers and given it to your stars. Thus the rule has become a self-fulfilling prophecy. And then what happens to your stars? The shine becomes less and less brilliant, they become less satisfied, engaged, and productive and — oops, they are moving towards the stinker end of the performance spectrum! Do not let that happen. You have a responsibility to expressly tell the employee, whether you think he should know better or not, that the performance level is not meeting expectations. You owe that to yourself, the employee, and the coworkers.

Correcting

So now you are at the point at which you have coached and counseled, and still the employee's performance is not meeting expectations. You have concluded it is time to issue corrective action. Here are a few things to consider.

Corrective versus Disciplinary Action

You may notice I used the term corrective rather than disciplinary action. I find the latter term still used in many employee handbooks. Neither term is good or bad nor right or wrong. I prefer corrective action because it focuses on the purpose of the action rather than on the person. It emphasizes the purpose, which is to correct behavior or to entice the employee to start or stop doing something. Disciplinary action may be read as a punitive term and seems to focus more on the person; e.g., it is punishment of the individual for a job not well done. If you agree and your company uses the latter term in its employee handbook, you might replace "discipline" and "disciplinary action" with "corrective action" next time you update your employee handbook. It's funny in a way. Sometimes a manager may ask me, usually after an employee has been coached and counseled multiple times and is being offered one last chance prior to termination, "But what if I issue discipline and the employee improves?" Isn't that the point? That question tells me there may be something more going on. Be honest with yourself and your employee. If the problem is more than just performance-based (like attitude) get to the heart of it, define it, and ensure all expectations are clear so the employee can meet them moving forward.

Equal versus Equitable Treatment

This topic was addressed in Chapter 1, but we will revisit it here. Have you ever had an employee tell you that your corrective action was unfair because the employee knows someone else who did the same thing but did not get "written up"? I suspect we all have. First, you know that it is quite likely that you did write the other employee up but this employee just does not know about it, as it should be. Second, and more to the point here, is that even if that is the case — e.g., another employee did do the same thing and did not get written up — so what? This is the difference between equal and equitable treatment. Most managers do not want to treat all their employees exactly the same nor do most employees want to be treated the same as all others, especially your top performers. What rising star wants to work under a compensation system that provides COLAs only and get the same pay increase as everyone else? What employee wants to be written up for excessive lateness when he is caring for a terminally ill child or family member (exclusive of FMLA leave, of course)? Treating employees equitably requires wise use of management discretion. It takes into account all the factors that come into play in any given scenario.

You may decide to not treat two employees equally; you may issue corrective action to one and not another. But that may not be inequitable because the two employees are not similarly situated (see Chapter 1).

Let me take a moment here to share some responses to the question above. What *do* you say when an employee tells you that you are not being fair because a coworker did the same thing and did not get written up? This might happen in the investigatory phase, as you are meeting with the employee to get his side of the story. Or you might hear it for the first time when you issue corrective action or give the employee anything less than an "Excellent" rating on his performance appraisal. How do you respond? I find a common response is "We're here to talk about you, not your coworker." That is true but sounds like you are closing the door and not open to a full investigation of all the facts. I prefer a response that lets the employee know that you heard him and will consider what he shared, and then redirects the employee back to the conversation at hand: "I hear that you think it's not fair because Christine did the same thing and I will look into that and address that with her if that is the case. For now, I want to focus on my expectations for you."

Regardless of what you call it, corrective action is generally formal in nature in that it involves a writing of some type that is placed in the employee's HR file. Some companies use a standard form that managers fill out; others simply use a memo-style approach. In either case, the written document then becomes a part of the employment record.

Employee Acknowledgement

I find a common question is whether the employer should provide a space for and/or require the employee to sign an acknowledgement that the employee has received the written notice of corrective action. There are some advantages and disadvantages regardless of which method you decide to use. Here is a brief, comparative review.

If you do not have a signature line for the employee to indicate his receipt of the form, you may create the opportunity for the employee to later claim, such as at an unemployment insurance (UI) or other administrative agency hearing, that the employee was never notified that he was not meeting expectations. You might overcome this by following a practice of always having another management-level witness present whenever you issue written, corrective action. The disadvantage of witnesses is that the employee could feel as if you or management were "ganging up" on him or not respecting the privacy of this "teachable moment." The decision of whether or not to have a witness is best made by you. You know your individual employees and for whom you are more likely than not to want a witness present. If you decide to not have a witness and also no signature, then you will bear the burden to show that the employee did, in fact, receive your written notice.

But having a signature line is not all a bed of roses either. How often have you had an employee refuse to sign? I suspect you are nodding yes right now. This is not uncommon. If the employee does not agree with the content or level of the corrective action, he may be inclined to not sign. Again, there is a strategy you might use to overcome this objection. For instance, on your performance appraisals, you may have a statement under the signature line that reads that the employee's signature does not necessarily indicate agreement with the appraisal but simply acknowledges his receipt of it. Still, even with that disclaimer, employees may still decline to sign the form.

This leads to the third issue as to whether the employer should make the signature a requirement of the corrective action or an option. I prefer the latter as it is usually better received by the employee. In this case, if the employee does not want to sign, the manager may simply write, "Employee declined to sign." I also prefer "declined" rather than "refused." The former is less confrontational. The offer to sign is an invitation, not a mandate, so the employee has the option to accept or decline your invitation to sign.

Managing Emotional Reactions

In any of these steps, particularly counseling and correcting, an employee may respond with one or more emotional reactions. Here are some tips for effectively managing your response to some of the more common emotional reactions.

Anger

Sometimes an employee may become angry when confronted with counseling on performance deficiencies. Your reaction can help de-escalate that emotion. Don't get drawn into the moment; watch the pace, pitch, and volume (PPV) of your own voice. The PPV of an angry person's voice usually increases; he speaks faster, at a higher pitch, and louder. Sometimes it can help to de-escalate this emotional reaction by doing just the opposite. Reduce the PPV of your own voice. Respond in a slow, low, and quiet tone of voice, with pauses between words such that the person may have to actually pause in his own frenetic pace of speech to listen to you. In that moment, you may recapture the person's attention and invite the person to take a break from the conversation and begin again in a few minutes or perhaps even in a few hours or the next day. How productive is the meeting at this point anyway? The emotion is likely overriding any productivity that could be derived from the meeting. How effective can you be when the person is focused on his own anger? Give the person time to return to a calm state before re-engaging him in the conversation. On another note, keep yourself safe. (See Chapter 5 for tips for avoiding certain legal claims like false imprisonment or intentional infliction of emotional distress, as well as for keeping yourself safe from a potentially violent employee.)

Denial or Blaming

Have you ever counseled an employee only to hear him accept no responsibility and state that the fault is not his but someone else's? As mentioned above, sometimes we may be compelled to tell the person that we are not there to discuss a coworker but to discuss this employee's performance. But if a coworker really is the source of a problem, the employee may hear that you are brushing off his very valid complaint. It may be appropriate to tell the employee that you will address those concerns momentarily and to then ask, before you do so, what responsibility this employee has, if any, for the concerns you have shared with him. The employee's answer will be important in determining the employee's willingness to be accountable, in any part, for the problem at hand. Even a small acknowledgement can go a long way.

For example, let's revisit our inventory control clerk from earlier in this chapter. His response to letting inventory levels fall below par is, "It's not my fault! Bob was on vacation so I couldn't get the requisition signed." We hear two issues here. The employee might not have the "R" in smart instructions. Asking him to maintain the par levels might not have been Realistic if he was constrained by not having the authority to sign off on a requisition or having another resource to do this for him. The second, however is his responsibility to ask for help. So we ask, "I understand you could not get the requisition signed because Bob was on vacation. So tell me what you could have done to have avoided this problem?" Now we cross our fingers and hope the employee recognizes the part he played by his own inaction. If not, then we point out, "If at any time you need something or have a problem getting your job done you need to let me know; doing nothing is not an acceptable response."

The other issues raised by the employee, however, should be addressed so you can determine whether or not they are valid concerns.

Silence

Humorist Josh Billings said, "Silence is one of the hardest arguments to refute."[10] And isn't this the truth? How do you engage an employee in a productive conversation when all he does is nod, shrug, and give an occasional "I dunno." You have probably heard about open- versus closed-ended questions. Here is a great time to try using open-ended questions. Rather than asking questions that can be answered with a "yes" or "no," ask questions that require a descriptive response. For example, a common question as we wrap up a meeting with an employee may be to ask, "Do you have any questions?" What does the employee almost always say? "No," a closed-ended response. Or you might ask, "Do you understand what I'm asking?" And, again, you get a closed-ended response, "Yes." But do you really know that the employee understands your expectations? An open-ended method for asking the same question would be to ask, "OK, just before we wrap up, tell me what you understand my expectation to be." This cannot be answered with a "yes" or "no" but requires the employee to repeat what he understands you want him to do. If you still get silence or a shrug, then you have the opportunity to again share the expectation and then ask the employee again, in an open-ended way, to tell you what he understands the expectation to be.

Another strategy for overcoming silence can be to offer the employee the opportunity to share his thoughts in writing. Some people just are not good orators; they are not comfortable telling you what is bothering them but could do so in writing. You might offer the employee the opportunity to think overnight about what you have shared and provide you with a written response the next day or by the end of the week.

Tears

Whether they are crocodile tears or real, this emotional reaction can be awkward to manage. First tip: always have a box of tissues in your office. There are few moments more awkward than when a tearful employee has no recourse but to wipe his nose on his sleeve. Keep the tissue box on your desk, rather than in a drawer, so the employee can take one rather than having to ask for one. Like managing anger, it may also be best to give the employee 5 to 10 minutes to collect himself and then return to the conversation. The question here may be where do you or the employee go during this interim period? That depends upon your office location as well as what is in your office. If you are an HR administrator with confidential files in your office that are unlocked, it may be best to invite the employee to step out and get a drink of water and return rather than leaving the employee alone in your office with access to files. On the other hand, if your office is in a highly trafficked hallway, telling the person to step out into a public area for all to see that he has been crying might not be wise either. Give these points consideration; you may decide that a meeting is best held in a neutral area such as a small conference room or vacant office space. That way, if a break is needed, you can tell the employee that you will step out, give the employee time to compose himself, and then return to continue the meeting.

Tears may also indicate that the employee is dealing with an issue unrelated to work that is personal in nature. If your company has an employee assistance program (EAP), this is a wonderful opportunity to remind the employee of this confidential resource if they need or would like someone else to talk to about work or personal matters that may be impacting work performance. Why do I say confidential? Remember that your EAP counselor is usually either a licensed social worker (LSW) or licensed clinical social worker (LCSW). That license gives the counselor a legal veil of confidentiality such that what the employee tells that counselor (barring a threat to self or others) is truly confidential. The EAP counselor may not disclose the information shared by the employee with the employer without the employee's consent. You, however, cannot provide an employee with absolute confidentiality, whether you are a manager, supervisor, or HR administrator. If you do refer an employee to the EAP, put a note on your calendar to follow up with the employee in a week or two. Tell the employee that you will do so, and then check in with the employee to see how things are going. It has been my experience that once the employee shares his story with the EAP counselor he may be much more comfortable and willing to share the same story with HR, the supervisor, or manager. Then you can determine what next steps, if any, to take to assist or help the employee.

This is also an opportunity to illustrate the value of HR and how HR can serve as a proverbial firewall for managers and supervisors. If HR has this type of conversation with the employee, personal and possibly protected information may be disclosed, such as information about a medical condition, issues with family members, or substance use/abuse. Too often, the disclosure of that information to a manager precedes corrective action. The employee then has a prima facia case to assert discrimination or retaliation for some protected status or activity.

For example, a manager is coaching an employee for unsatisfactory work performance: reports have repeatedly been submitted late and with errors despite previous coaching. When the employee becomes emotional and cries, the supervisor refers her to the EAP. HR then follows up. In the meeting with HR the employee shares that the EAP was a great resource for her. Her family is having some serious financial issues, she recently filed for bankruptcy, and she found out she was pregnant. Put together it was all just overwhelming her. In the interim, she has turned in another report late and with multiple errors; the supervisor issues corrective action. Since the supervisor has no knowledge of the employee's bankruptcy or pregnancy, it would be very difficult for the employee to assert that she is being discriminated against on either of those bases.

Passive-Aggressive

This pattern of behavior may be less gently referred to as being two-faced. This behavior is demonstrated by the employee who is very reticent, polite, and apologetic in your presence, indicating that he is sorry and will do better moving forward. After the employee leaves your office, however, you begin to hear from coworkers that he is complaining about you and the company and unfair treatment, and generally bad-mouthing the organization behind your back. What do you do? Ask the employee about it. You may simply tell him that it has come to your attention that he may be complaining about you or the company. Can you guess what the employee's first question often is? That's right, "Who told you that?" There is no need to disclose that to the employee. Notice that I indicated you would tell the employee that it has come to your attention that he "may be" complaining. You may simply tell him that who told you is not important; what is important is that he understands that such behavior is not acceptable. Remind the employee of the company's appropriate resources for expressing concerns (e.g., the employee's supervisor, human resources, EAP, confidential hotline). Then advise the employee that if you continue to receive such reports and you find that he is, in fact, engaging in such behavior, it may result in corrective action. Let him know that venting to coworkers and contaminating workplace morale is not acceptable. Here's another common question: "But doesn't that violate the employee's right to freedom of speech?" Remember that freedom of speech is a constitutional matter applicable only to the public sector or government as an employer, not the private sector. And for those of you reading this book and who work in the public sector, even the U.S. Supreme Court has held, "The first amendment does not require a public office to be run as a roundtable for employee complaints over internal office affairs."[11]

Practical Tips

- Why wait until the employee is onboard? Begin setting expectations in your job interviews; tell candidates about your company's culture, work ethic, core values and your general departmental expectations.
- Don't presume understanding. Use the skills described in this chapter to ensure the employee understands your expectations. Give SMART instructions and ask open-ended questions.
- Don't procrastinate! Do not put off until tomorrow what you can do today. I have seen it happen time and again when a manager puts off coaching, counseling, or correcting, and just as he finally decides to take some type of action, the employee expresses a need for FMLA leave or military leave, files a workers' compensation claim, or informs the employer she is pregnant — in other words,

indicates some protected status or activity that could now make the corrective action look like retaliation.

- Let HR serve as a firewall for managers and supervisors. Remember that you cannot discriminate against what you do not know. So when it comes to personal issues and information about employees, it is best to be shared with HR or the EAP counselor than the employee's direct manager, supervisor, or any person in the employee's chain of command.

4

Employee, Where Art Thou? Managing Disability and Leave Issues

On March 12, 2012, I had the honor of testifying on behalf of the Society for Human Resource Management (SHRM) before the U.S. Senate Committee on Health, Education, Labor and Pensions hearing on stay-at-work and back-to-work strategies in the private sector. I explained, as I suspect you will agree, that employers are becoming more learned and creative in providing flexible staffing models including:

1. Flex time — permitting employees to work flexible schedules around a "core" set of hours.
2. Compressed work schedules (CWS) and alternative work schedules (AWS) — such as a 4-10 workweek or 8-9-8 pay period in which during the first 8 days of a two-week pay period an employee works 9 hours a day, then 8 hours the next day and is off the last day, usually every other Friday.
3. Job sharing — where two employees may share the duties and work schedule of one full-time equivalent or FTE.
4. Teleworking — permitting employees to work from home or an alternate location.

But life for business owners, managers, and HR professionals is hectic, and navigating the maze of laws with limited resources and personnel can be overwhelming. Despite their merits, the Americans with Disabilities Act (ADA), Family and Medical Leave Act (FMLA), and workers' compensation laws are sometimes referred to as "the Bermuda

Triangle of HR." They can be particularly complex, overlapping, and frustrating for employers to administer. Towards the close of the hearing, Senator Tom Harkin, the committee chairman, asked, "Why don't employers do more to help employees stay at work and return to work?" My answer simply put was that as employers we sometimes walk on eggshells, afraid to say or do the wrong thing so sometimes we do nothing instead. This chapter will focus on some of those legal complexities and issues that seem to give rise, more often than not, to litigation, as well as frustrated employee relations.

The Americans with Disabilities Act

Since the first edition of this book the Americans with Disabilities Act (ADA) celebrated its 25th anniversary, on July 26, 2015. To recognize the event, the U.S. Equal Employment Opportunity Commission (EEOC) dedicated a webpage[1] to provide current information and updates for employers and employees.

The ADA generally covers employers with 15 or more employees. The law prohibits discrimination against a qualified individual who has a present disability or a history of a disability; who is perceived to have a disability (even if the perception is wrong); or who has a relationship with or associates with an individual with a disability. A disability is defined as a physical or mental impairment that substantially limits one or more major life activities. The ADA covers your current employees, former employees, and applicants. It is important to note that the law protects qualified individuals with disabilities. A qualified individual is one who can perform the essential functions of a job with or without a reasonable accommodation.

The law also requires a covered employer, if needed and absent undue hardship, to provide a reasonable accommodation to a qualified individual with a disability so the individual can perform the essential functions of the job. Reasonable accommodation is defined as, "(i) Modifications or adjustments to a job application process that enable a qualified applicant with a disability to be considered for the position such qualified applicant desires; or (ii) Modifications or adjustments to the work environment, or to the manner or circumstances under which the position held or desired is customarily performed, that enable a qualified individual with a disability to perform the essential functions of that position; or (iii) Modifications or adjustments that enable a covered entity's employee with a disability to enjoy equal benefits and privileges of employment as are enjoyed by its other similarly situated employees without disabilities."

The federal regulations consider five elements to determine whether an accommodation would impose an undue hardship:

1. The nature and net cost of the accommodation needed, taking into consideration the availability of tax credits and deductions, and/or outside funding;

2. The overall financial resources of the facility or facilities involved in the provision of the reasonable accommodation, the number of persons employed at such facility, and the effect on expenses and resources;

3. The overall financial resources of the covered entity, the overall size of the business of the covered entity with respect to the number of its employees, and the number, type, and location of its facilities;

4. The type of operation or operations of the covered entity, including the composition, structure, and functions of the workforce of such entity, and the geographic separateness and administrative or fiscal relationship of the facility or facilities in question to the covered entity; and

5. The impact of the accommodation upon the operation of the facility, including the impact on the ability of other employees to perform their duties and the impact on the facility's ability to conduct business.[2]

So, for example, a likely reasonable accommodation may be for an employee who works on a loading dock and due to a medical condition needs a hydraulic hand jack that costs $300 to help him lift boxes weighing more than 50 pounds up to and down from the loading platform. If the employee needed a piece of equipment that cost $3,000, then that may also be reasonable for a larger employer but may not be for a smaller employer with fewer financial resources. The key is to remember that this analysis must be done on a case-by-case basis, and the outcome could be different for one location, site, or facility as compared to another location, site, or facility of the same employer or different employers.

Leave can also be a reasonable accommodation. On May 9, 2016, the EEOC published new guidance called "Employer-Provided Leave and the Americans with Disabilities Act."[3] The introduction reads in part, "some employers may not know that they may have to modify policies that limit the amount of leave employees can take when an employee needs additional leave as a reasonable accommodation." In 2009 a federal court approved the largest monetary amount ever in a single EEOC ADA suit as a result, in part of an inflexible leave exhaustion policy.[4]

Similarly, the guidance reminds us that, "employer policies that require employees on extended leave to be 100 percent healed or able to work without restrictions may deny some employees reasonable accommodations that would enable them to return to work."

In addition to legal and regulatory compliance and maintaining positive employee relations, employers may reap other rewards and be eligible for certain tax credits[5] for making workplaces more accessible to persons with disabilities such as:

- The Small Business Tax Credit (Internal Revenue Code Section 44: Disabled Access Credit).
- The Work Opportunity Tax Credit (Internal Revenue Code Section 51).
- The Architectural/Transportation Tax Deduction (Internal Revenue Code Section 190 Barrier Removal).

Employers should be aware of some ancillary guidance published by the EEOC that impact ADA practices and compliance:

2016: ADA and GINA: Applicability of Incentive Limits for Employer Wellness Programs[6]

The final rule says employers may provide limited financial and other incentives in exchange for an employee answering disability-related questions or taking medical examinations as part of a wellness program, whether or not the program is part of a health plan. There are certain caps or limits on the incentive that can be offered, wellness programs must be reasonable designed and voluntary, and more. The rule stipulates that employers are required to provide their employees with particular notice.[7] The rule notes there may also be other compliance issues for wellness programs as they related to the Health Insurance Portability and Accountability Act (HIPAA), the Genetic Information Nondiscrimination Act (GINA), and more.

2015: EEOC Enforcement Guidance on Pregnancy Discrimination and Related Issues[8]

While pregnancy itself is not a disability, pregnant workers and job applicants are not excluded from the protections of the ADA. Changes to the definition of the term "disability" resulting from enactment of the ADA Amendments Act of 2008 (ADAAA) make it much easier for pregnant workers with pregnancy-related impairments to demonstrate that they have disabilities for which they may be entitled to a reasonable accommodation under the ADA. Most of this revised guidance remains the same as the prior version. Some noteworthy changes include those made to sections relating to disparate treatment and light duty in response to the U.S. Supreme Court's decision in *Young v. United Parcel Serv., Inc.,* 575 U.S.___, 135 S.Ct. 1338 (2014).[9]

With regard to disparate treatment, an employer will be found to have discriminated on the basis of pregnancy if an employee's pregnancy, childbirth, or related medical condition was all or part of the motivation for an employment decision. The guidance clarifies that discriminatory motive may be established directly, or it can be inferred from the surrounding facts and circumstances. An example of such evidence could be an employer policy or practice that, although not discriminatory on its face, significantly burdens pregnant employees and cannot be supported by a sufficiently strong justification. The U.S. Supreme Court said in the case cited above that evidence of an employer policy or practice of providing light duty to a large percentage of non-pregnant employees while failing to provide light duty to a large percentage of pregnant workers might establish that the policy or practice significantly burdens pregnant employees. If the employer's reasons for its actions are not sufficiently strong to justify the burden, that will "give rise to an inference of intentional discrimination."[10]

With regard to light duty, when there is no direct evidence of discrimination a plaintiff must produce evidence that a similarly situated worker was treated differently or more favorably than the pregnant worker to establish a prima facie case of discrimination. The guidance clarifies that the similarly situated worker need not be similar in all but the protected way. The plaintiff could satisfy her prima facie burden by identifying an employee who was similar in his or her ability or inability to work due to an impairment (e.g., an employee with a lifting restriction) and who was provided an accommodation that the pregnant employee sought and was denied.

Proactive employers may periodically peruse the EEOC's website for recent guidance[11] and seek guidance from their legal counsel.

Family and Medical Leave Act

SHRM reports that of all the questions received by it on HR and related issues, the highest volume is FMLA questions. The good news for employers is that the DOL reports that the number of claims filed alleging FMLA violations decreased every year from 2011 to 2016.[12] The primary violation is termination, followed by discrimination then refusal to grant leave. While the basic tenets and provisions of the FMLA have not changed through the regulatory process since 2008, there are administrative agency interpretations, updates, and guidance of which employers should be aware.

In June 2015, the U.S. Department of Labor (DOL) issued a 20-page publication, "The Employee's Guide to the Family and Medical Leave Act."[13] The guide provides information to employees on:

- Who can use FMLA leave?
- When can I use FMLA leave?
- What can the FMLA do for me?
- How do I request FMLA leave?

- Communication with your employer
- Medical certification
- Returning to work
- How to file a complaint
- Website resources

Not to leave employers out, in 2016 the DOL published a some-what more comprehensive, 76-page guide for employers — you guessed it — "The Employer's Guide to the Family and Medical Leave Act." The law still provides up to 12 workweeks of job-protected leave in a 12-month period to an eligible employee and still generally applies to employers with 50 or more employees. An employer may still choose any 12-month period it prefers such as calendar year, fiscal year, or back-ward- or forward-rolling year. (Note that a separate 12-month period is specifically defined, however, for military caregiver leave; see below). The employer, however must give employees notice of the 12-month period it chooses, such as in its FMLA policy, which is required to be incorporated into the employer's employee handbook if it has one. An eligible employee continues to retain the right to be reinstated to the job he had when he began covered leave upon returning from FMLA leave within the 12-week period. The following is intended to provide only a high-level overview of just some of the key aspects of the FMLA as it is administered today.

Which Employers Are Covered Under the FMLA?

As mentioned above, employers that employ 50 or more employees are generally FMLA-covered employers. Coverage, however, does not apply on the very first day that an employer hires its 50th employee nor does coverage end of the same day an employer should fall below the 50-em-ployee threshold. Let's say an FMLA-covered employer implemented a reduction in force 30 days ago. The employer now employs only 40 em-ployees. Today an employee asks for FMLA leave. Is the employer an FMLA-covered employer today since it no longer employs at least 50 employees? It depends. It is important to remember that the definition of a covered employer is one that employs 50 or more employees for each working day during each of 20 or more calendar workweeks in the current or preceding calendar year. If, in the example above, the employer implemented its reduction in force (RIF) on June 1, then it would still be an FMLA-covered employer in this calendar year *and* the next calendar year (the 20th week of each year generally falls in May). On the flip side, if today an employer hires its 50th employee, it will not be an FMLA-covered employer until it has met the definition described above.

Which Employees Are Eligible for FMLA Leave?

Eligible employees are still those that have worked for your company for a total of 12 months. Those 12 months need not be consecutive but must have occurred within the last seven years with some exceptions, such as absences for covered military service. For example, if an employee works for you for seven full months in this calendar year, resigns, and returns five years later and works for you for five full months, then that employee would have met the length-of-service requirements. In addition, however, the eligible employee must have also worked for your company for at least 1,250 hours within the immediately preceding 12 months. So, in the example above, the requirement for hours worked may not yet have been met (assuming full-time employment for five months, the employee might have worked only 21 weeks for 840 hours). But if the employee had worked for two full months initially and has now, five years later, worked for you for the last 10 full months on a full-time basis, then he probably has met the hours-of-service requirement. The eligible employee must also meet a third requirement: he must work at a site that employs at least 50 employees at or within 75 miles of that site. For example, let's say a financial institution has 125 employees. Forty employees work at the main office and the rest work at branches scattered throughout the state. If no branch, including the corporate office, is located within 75 miles of any other branch and no branch employs at least 50 employees, is any employee eligible for FMLA? No. While the financial institution may be an FMLA-covered employer, no employee is eligible because none works at a location that employs at least 50 employees at or within 75 miles. But the federal regulations require that covered employer to still post the FMLA notice in the workplace even though it has no eligible employees.[14]

Reasons Eligible Employee May Take FMLA Leave

Leave is still provided for:

1. The birth and care of the newborn child of an employee.
2. Placement with the employee of a child for adoption or foster care.
3. The care of an immediate family member (spouse, child under age 18 or otherwise incapable of self-care, or parent) with a serious health condition.
4. When the employee is unable to work because of his own serious health condition. Over the last several years and since the first edition of this book there have been some changes and clarification provided for some of these terms.

On January 14, 2013, the DOL indicated that additional guidance was needed regarding the definition of "son or daughter" as it applies to an employee seeking to take FMLA leave to care for a son or daughter with a disability who is 18 years of age or older. An Administrator's Interpretation (AI)[15] clarified that the age of a son or daughter at the onset of a disability is not relevant in determining a parent's entitlement to FMLA leave

Effective March 27, 2015, the DOL changed its definition of "spouse" for FMLA purposes. The DOL moved from a "state of residence" rule to a "place of celebration" rule. The definition of spouse now looks to the law of the place in which the marriage was entered into, as opposed to the law of the state in which the employee resides. A place of celebration rule allows all legally married couples, whether opposite-sex or same-sex, or married under common law, to have consistent federal family leave rights regardless of where they live. The definition of spouse expressly includes individuals in lawfully recognized same-sex and common-law marriages and marriages that were validly entered into outside of the United States if they could have been entered into in at least one state.

In addition, there are military leave provisions:

Military Caregiver Leave. FMLA protections are now provided for employees who need to provide care for a family member who is a covered service member of the armed forces, including a member of the National Guard or Reserves, or a member of the armed forces, the National Guard, or Reserves who is on the temporary disability retired list, who has a serious injury or illness incurred in the line of duty on active duty for which he is undergoing medical treatment, recuperation, or therapy; or otherwise in outpatient status; or otherwise on the temporary disability retired list. For purposes of this leave, a family member includes spouse, son or daughter (of any age), or parent, or next of kin of a covered service member. A veteran who is undergoing medical treatment, recuperation, or therapy for a serious injury or illness is a covered veteran if he or she:

1. Was a member of the Armed Forces (including a member of the National Guard or Reserves).
2. Was discharged or released under conditions other than dishonorable.
3. Was discharged within the five-year period before the eligible employee first takes FMLA military caregiver leave to care for the veteran.

Eligible employees are able to take up to 26 workweeks of leave in a 12-month period, inclusive of FMLA leave taken for other qualifying reasons. This 12-month period is specifically defined as starting from the first day leave is taken to care for a covered service member, so an employer may have to run two FMLA "clocks" for one employee: the 12-month period it has chosen for other types of FMLA leave (fiscal, calendar, backward-rolling) and this 12-month period.

Leave for Qualifying Exigencies for Families of Military Members. Eligible employees may also take FMLA leave to address certain qualifying exigencies for the employee's spouse, son, daughter, or parent who is a military member on covered active duty. The definition of covered military members includes those serving in the Regular Armed Forces on covered active duty, as well as the National Guard and Reserves. This also includes a foreign country deployment requirement. Qualifying exigencies are defined as:

1. Short-notice deployment.
2. Military events and related activities.
3. Child care and school activities.
4. Financial and legal arrangements.
5. Counseling.
6. Rest and recuperation.
7. Post-deployment activities.
8. Additional activities where the employer and employee agree to the leave.

Some other common questions and points of clarification include:

What notice must an employer provide to an employee and when and what is the penalty for failing to do so? A covered employer must provide an employee with the "Notice of Eligibility and Rights" within five days from the time the employer learns of the employee's need for FMLA leave. If an employee suffers individual harm because the employer did not follow the notification rules and provided the notice more than five days later, the employer may be liable for damages. (See the Practical Tips at the end of this chapter; your managers are often critical in this part of the process.)

In addition to the first "Notice of Eligibility and Rights," the employer must next provide the employee with a "Designation Notice" within five days from the date the employer determines whether the need for leave is FMLA qualifying. Practically speaking, this is usually the date the employee returns the FMLA medical certification form. This raises a common question: "What if an employee tells me that he does not want his qualifying leave to be counted as FMLA leave?" Under the FMLA, the employer retains the right to designate qualifying leave as FMLA. If the employer does not, then the employee may retain the right to a full 12 workweeks of FMLA leave, despite having already taken time off from work that qualifies for FMLA leave.

What notice must an employee provide to his employer? Where an employee's need for FMLA leave is foreseeable, which is not the case in most instances in my experience, then the employee must provide the employer with at least 30 days of notice. If the employee's need for leave is not foreseeable within 30 days, then the employee is required to give his employer notice as soon as is practicable. An employer may require an employee to comply with the employer's usual and customary notice and procedural requirements for requesting leave, absent unusual circumstances. For example, if an employer has a policy that an employee must call his supervisor regarding any absence, then the employee taking FMLA leave may be required to do the same; e.g., telling a coworker to tell his supervisor that he will be absent may not be acceptable.

If an eligible employee requests FMLA leave for surgery that requires and/or results in an overnight stay in the hospital but the surgery is elective, is it covered under the FMLA? The answer is yes, it may be covered. The federal regulations read, "Conditions for which cosmetic treatments are administered (such as most treatments for acne or plastic surgery) are not 'serious health conditions' unless inpatient hospital care is required or unless complications develop."[16]

What is the definition of a serious health condition? The current regulations still define a serious health condition as one that involves either inpatient care or continuing treatment by a health care provider. Let's walk through a couple of examples.

Q: If an employee is absent from work for three consecutive days and does not see a doctor, does that qualify for FMLA leave?

A: Possibly not. The absence must be for more than three consecutive days or of a shorter period of time but intermittent and as a result of the same chronic health condition and, in either case, must include treatment by a health care provider.

Q: So what if the employee is out for four consecutive days and calls his doctor, who puts him on a regimen of aspirin? Does that qualify as FMLA leave?

A: Possibly not. The employee must have at least one in-person visit with the health care provider in order for the leave to qualify as FMLA leave and that visit must take place within seven days of the first day of incapacity. Generally, a regimen that includes over-the-counter medications such as aspirin, antihistamines, or salves, or bed-rest, drinking fluids, exercise, and other similar activities that can be initiated without a visit to a health care provider, is not, by itself, sufficient to constitute a regimen of continuing treatment for purposes of FMLA leave.

Q: If the employee is never out for more than three consecutive days but is intermittently absent for a day or two here and there, does that qualify for FMLA leave?

A: In the case of intermittent absences for a chronic health condition like asthma or migraine headaches, the absences must also include periodic visits (defined as at least twice a year) for treatment by a health care provider, or by a nurse under direct supervision of a health care provider.

Does "light duty" work count towards FMLA? Generally not. Under the current regulations, time an employee spends working in a "light duty" position does not count against an employee's FMLA leave entitlement. But, this is balanced with a provision that the employee's right to reinstatement ends in the FMLA year used by the employer. So let's assume an employer uses the backward-rolling calendar year for FMLA purposes, which is what I find most employers use. An employee goes out on FMLA leave on June 1, but the employee is released to work light-duty eight weeks later. You have a light-duty position available and the employee accepts your offer, but the physician indicates that the duration of the need for light-duty is unknown at this time. Does the employer have to permit the employee to work in that light-duty position for more than the four remaining weeks of FMLA leave? Yes, because the time spent working in the light-duty position does not count against the employee's FMLA leave entitlement. So does the employer have to permit the employee to continue working in that light-duty position forever? No, the employee's right to be reinstated to his job expires on

May 31 of the following year, which is the end of the FMLA year that his employer uses.

Does an employee who is absent on FMLA leave still have the right to bonuses and awards, like a perfect attendance award? Not necessarily. Today, an employer may deny a bonus or perfect attendance award to an employee who took FMLA leave — but only if the employer treats employees taking non-FMLA leave in an identical way. The perfect attendance example is pretty easy: as long as only those employees who incurred zero absences receive the award, then the employee who was absent under FMLA may be denied the award. But what about bonuses? What if an employer offers a pay-for-performance bonus program and an employee fails to meet a sales or productivity standard because he was absent on FMLA? Can the employee be denied this bonus? The answer is the same: yes, so long as other employees who missed the standard, regardless of the reason, are also denied the bonus. If a bonus or other payment is based on the achievement of a specified goal, such as hours worked, products sold, or perfect attendance, and the employee has not met the goal due to FMLA leave, then the payment may be denied, unless otherwise paid to employees on an equivalent leave status for a reason that does not qualify as FMLA leave.

May an employer contact an employee's physician to get more information? The FMLA works in conjunction with the Health Insurance Portability and Accountability Act (HIPAA) medical privacy rule applicable to communications between employers and employees' health care providers. FMLA regulations limit who may contact the health care provider and bans an employee's direct supervisor from making the contact. Here are two common scenarios:

In the first scenario, you receive an employee's medical certification form and part of it is unclear to you. It's not unclear in the sense that you cannot read it, but you need clarification. Take the case of a medical certification that indicates, "The employee will need to rest periodically throughout the day." What does that mean? How many times per day will he need to rest and for how long each time? For what duration will this limitation last? In this instance, the employer must first give the employee an opportunity to provide more complete information within seven days.

If the employee is unable or unwilling, then the employer is permitted to contact the employee's physician directly and simply ask for "clarification." The employer is to *not* request any additional medical information but to simply ask for clarification of the information already provided.

The second scenario is similar to, but different from, the example above. This time let's say the medical certification form is clear and you understand it, but it appears that it may not be valid. Perhaps it is completed in two different colors of ink, in two different handwriting styles, or perhaps there are some smudges or cross-outs and it appears that some information was changed. You want the employee's physician to authenticate the form; that is, you want the employee's physician to confirm that he did, in fact, complete the entire form as you see it. In this instance, the same rule as described above applies.

In either instance, for clarification or authentication, the question arises as to who may contact the employee's physician. To make such contact, the employer must use a health care provider, an HR professional, a leave administrator, or a management official. Under no circumstances, however, may the employee's direct supervisor contact the employee's health care provider.

Military Leave

The Uniformed Services Employment and Reemployment Rights Act (USERRA) is a federal law that provides certain employment protections to individuals called to serve in the uniformed services, including active and inactive training. The DOL offers online training programs to introduce employers to the rules and regulations surrounding USERRA.[17] There are two issues I see commonly arise and of which employers should be aware. First, there are the reinstatement rights of persons returning from covered service. Most employers seem to know that covered individuals generally have the right to be reinstated to their job for up to five years (with exceptions). Some employers, however, are not aware of the "escalator clause." Unlike FMLA, which requires reinstatement to the job the employee had when he went out on leave, USERRA provides that the covered employee shall be reinstated to the job he would have had had the employee not gone out on covered military leave. That means the employee should be reinstated to the position he had when he left plus any promotions, pay increases, enhanced benefits, etc., that the employee would reasonably have been expected to receive had the employee not gone out on leave.

The second matter is related to continued employment. In Chapter 6, we talk about at-will employment, and even if you have not yet read that chapter, I suspect you know what that is. Employment at-will simply means that the employment relationship continues only at the will of both parties; either party may terminate the employment relationship at any time, for any reason, with or without notice. But when an employee returns from USERRA covered service of more than 30 days, that employee is no longer an at-will employee for either six months or one year, depending upon how long the employee served in the uniformed services. The employee may not be discharged except for cause. For example, let's say a company has a reduction in force (RIF) policy that is based on seniority; e.g., the last hired are the first laid off (LIFO — last in, first out). A company is experiencing serious financial difficulties and finds that it must implement a RIF. In accordance with its policy, it plans to abolish the positions of the last 10 people hired, one of whom is an employee who was reinstated three months ago after returning from covered service. Can the employer RIF this employee? The answer is most likely "No." The company must go to the 11th person on the list.

You should also check the laws in your states of operation; many have laws that provide certain rights and protections for individuals called to service in the state militia.

Court Appearances — Jury/Witness Leave

There are currently no federal laws that require employers to give leave to individuals called to appear in court; many states do have such laws, however. I find the more common rights are related to jury service and witness leave, particularly for victims of domestic violence. Some state laws provide that an employee's absence to serve on a jury or for any other protected leave may not be the sole reason for adverse action, such as issuing corrective action or terminating employment; others provide that an employee may not be subject to any adverse employment action for such service, whether it is the sole reason or not. Yet others expand that protection to include those who are summoned as a witness. Some require that the time off be paid, others do not.

Voting Leave

As of this writing there is also currently no federal law that requires employers to provide leave for individuals to vote. At least 29 states, however, require employers to provide employees with time off from work to vote,[18] and some states qualify that time off must be granted only if the employee is not already scheduled time off from work for some minimum period of time such as one to two hours while the polls are open. Some states require employers to provide time off from work to vote and that the time off must be paid.

Parental Leave

Other than the FMLA, as of this writing there is no federal law that requires employers to provide time off for parental leave. But there has been federal legislation pending that proposed to do so. Work-life balance has been a "hot" topic for several years now and is getting national attention. For example, the Healthy Families Act has been introduced over several years to require employers to provide paid sick time so their employees can address their own health needs and the health needs of their families.[19] The trend is more prolific at the state level. As of this writing a handful of states have enacted laws requiring certain employers to offer paid sick or related leave to full and/or part time employees with more states considering comparable, pending legislation.[20] Whether you are an HR professional, business owner, or manager reading this book, membership in SHRM and/or an affiliated, local chapter in your state can provide you with regular legislative updates so you can monitor federal and state legislation. You might also check to see if your company belongs to your local or state chamber of commerce. These, too, are often great resources for tracking legislation. Once again, many states and local jurisdictions have laws that do provide certain leave, paid or unpaid, for employees who need to take time off from work for a variety of related reasons, such as to care for an immediate family member, to attend a child's school-related activity, and more. Be sure you are familiar with those covering your business operations.

Practical Tips

- Train your management team members. They do not have to know all the details or ins-and-outs of the FMLA, ADA, and the myriad other leave laws. But they are on the front line and are generally the first to know if an employee has a qualifying absence or condition. Too often we hear stories of an HR administrator who hears for the first time from a supervisor that an employee has been absent from work for several weeks. At that point, the employer may have already failed to provide the FMLA notice in a timely manner (within five days). It can be a proactive practice to train managers regarding some initial "bells and whistles" that can alert them as to when they should contact human resources or the company's leave administrator.

- Develop your policies. Whether you use the DOL's sample policy or have created your own, define the year in which your employees may take up to 12 workweeks of leave; e.g., calendar, fiscal or backward rolling. Many employers use the latter as it is most advantageous to the employer. The federal regulations provide that where an employer fails to select a specific 12-month period, the option that provides the most beneficial outcome for the employee will be used. For example, let's say you intended to use the backward-rolling year but your policy was silent. An employee then uses 12 weeks of FMLA leave from October through December. On January 1, the employee requests an additional 12 weeks of leave. While you might reply that the employee had exhausted all 12 weeks and will not be eligible again until October of the current year, the employee might say, in accordance with the federal regulations, that since your policy was silent the employee is eligible for another 12 weeks with the start of the new calendar year, effectively giving the employee 24 weeks of job-protected leave in a six-month period.

- Review your EEO and harassment policies. If they do not already include disability — as well as other legally protected categories such as race, religion, sex, and national origin — consider adding it. If your policies do not already include prohibiting discrimination and harassment on the basis of a person's perceived disability as well as their association with a person with a disability, consider adding those as well.

- Clearly address employee eligibility by including the reference to working at a site that employs 50 or more employees at or within 75 miles. If you do not do so, then employees working at smaller sites may read the policy, request FMLA leave and then become quite frustrated or disappointed when told they are not eligible. If that happens, you may have not just an employee relations issue on your hands but a court may hold that your policy created an express or implied contract and, absent the clarifying term to the definition of eligibility, you may be obligated to grant FMLA leave to that employee.

- If your company has employment practices liability insurance (EPLI), check with your carrier to determine if they will give your company a discount if it has a specific ADA policy in the employee handbook and/or conducts an HR compliance audit. If your company does not carry EPLI coverage, then you may want to contact several insurance carriers to get quotes to compare.

- Consider joining a professional or trade association (you or your company) such as SHRM, a chamber of commerce, or an industry-specific trade or professional organization that can help you stay abreast of changing laws and regulations, particularly if your company is a multi-state employer.

- Know your state and local laws. Again, many states have laws that require employers to provide a certain amount of leave, paid or unpaid, to employees for family, medical, military, voting, and other reasons. Unfortunately for employers, sometimes local jurisdictions within the state have a similar law but with conflicting requirements. Navigating that maze, developing HR and payroll systems that track the information needed and help you maintain required records can be challenging at best. Network with industry and other colleagues to share best practices and ensure that not just your policy but your practices comply with federal and state law requirements.

5

Maintaining an Inclusive Workplace

The Business Case

The more I see, read, hear, and talk about this topic, the more I am led to conclude that there are inseparable connections between workplace civility, inclusion, and employee engagement. Research shows actively engaged employees are more productive employees; that's good for the employer and the employee. I find Dale Carnegie's data powerful, for example "companies with engaged employees outperform those without by up to 202%." Even more powerful to me, perhaps, is the direct correlation that the relationship an employee has with his direct supervisor has on engagement: 80 percent of employees dissatisfied with their direct manager were disengaged.[1]

Articles tout ways employers can use employee engagement to create a more inclusive workplace; others extol how maintaining an inclusive workplace fosters employee engagement. To the former, a Gallup study in 2016 found "gender diversity predicted the financial success of business units in two independent companies. The combination of employee engagement and gender diversity resulted in 46% to 58% higher financial performance — comparable revenue and net profit, respectively ..."[2] To the latter, Deloitte published work in 2015 that found:

1. Statistically, diversity practices relate positively to employee engagement.
2. There are strong causal linkages between diversity, trust, and employee engagement.

3. Perceptions of inclusion are an important moderating factor in diversity, creating trust and therefore driving employee engagement.[3]

4. I particularly like the Deloitte findings, as they include the trust factor. But what are we talking about? The concepts seem simple enough. Yet why do we so often deal with employee relations issues that involve contrary behavior: mean, rude derogatory conduct between coworkers, colleagues, supervisors, and managers? I have no answer to that question. I could go off on a tangent here, taking a look at the world around us fraught with incivility from politics to media ads and so much more. But let's not. Let's stick to the workplace; that is, after all, why I'm writing and you are reading this book.

People, Perception, and Communication

The first edition of this book spent some time in this chapter addressing, "People, Perception and Communication." We should never ever lose the human side of our working relationships. I find myself saying more frequently to unhappy and dissatisfied employees, "Life is too short. We spend way too much time at work. Don't work at a place where you're not happy." But what about the people who are the cause of that unhappiness? What do we do with the coworkers and managers who are at the heart of the angst, the bullies? What do they do with themselves?!

Sometimes big gains come from small actions. Consider the following:

Presumptive inquiries — Someone asks you, "What's wrong?" You were in a fine mood, feeling good … until now. You reply, "Nothing. What's wrong with you?" Rather than asking a question that has the presumption in it, just modify the question to leave out the presumption, "How ya doin'?" or "How's it goin'?"

Statements of exclusion — An employee asks a coworker, "You don't want to go out to lunch with us, do you?" The coworker thinks, "I guess not now!" Not only does the question have a presumption in it but asked in the negative it is not very inviting!

Statements of assumption — "She wouldn't want to come out after work; she has kids." Now, I don't have kids, but I know plenty of people who do and it seems to me there are times they need a drink more than I!

You really can't make these things up. This is what we hear from employees regarding comments made to them by coworkers, colleagues, and — yes, sometimes their manager or supervisor.

Managers! Be the eyes and ears of your organization. Remember the hall monitor when you were in school (excuse me, do I date myself here?) You are the climate monitor. Keep your finger on the pulse of employee relations. Share gentle reminders for staff to invite team members who are usually not active participants into the group. Of course everyone cannot do everything together all the time. And maybe the coworker will meet your expectation and decline the invitation. But I can think of *so many* occasions when I have been called to facilitate poor employee relationships and this is what I hear. It is the mere fact that someone has not been included that they feel intentionally excluded.

So with that as our foundation you recognize that it is your role to encourage open and appropriate dialogue between employees. It is also your responsibility, whether you are a manager, supervisor, or HR professional, to monitor the workplace, maintain positive employee relations, and prevent and correct unlawful harassment.

So what *is* unlawful workplace harassment and what are the current trends? What is it *not*?

First, I assume that anyone reading this book has most likely taken some type of harassment training somewhere in their career. As a result, this chapter assumes you know the basics of unlawful harassment, particularly sexual harassment, so we won't cover that. What we will cover are some of the latest trends, tips, tools, and reminders for proactive practices.

What *Is* Unlawful Harassment?

Remember that there is a wide range of unkind, uncivil, inappropriate, and unprofessional behavior that is not unlawful harassment. It is, however, more likely than not that such behavior is a violation of your company's policy or code of conduct. The U.S. EEOC website reminds us that, "Petty slights, annoyances, and isolated incidents (unless extremely serious) will not rise to the level of illegality[4] … the law doesn't prohibit simple teasing, off-hand comments, or isolated incidents that are not very serious."[5] To constitute unlawful harassment, remember that the behavior complained of must be based on a person's membership in a legally protected class. This may also include if an individual is perceived to be a member of a legally protected class, even if the perception is wrong or if the person is discriminated against or harassment based upon his association with a person on the basis of *that* person's legally protected class. For example, let's say an employee reports that his supervisor is harassing him. When asked to explain what is happening, the employee describes close and constant supervision, being counseled every time he is just a few minutes late for work, and being constantly reminded about performance errors. Is this descriptive of unlawful harassment? Not based on the description above. It sounds like the employee is not performing satisfactorily, and, while he may feel harassed, it is not unlawful. What is missing to constitute unlawful harassment? Some indication that the manager is treating this employee differently from other employees who are similarly situated and that difference in treatment is based on the employee's membership in a protected class. Try the next scenario.

Now let's spin that fact pattern: Now the employee describes his harassment the same as above and adds that he is aware of female coworkers who also come in late, have an error rate equal to or greater than his, but who are not constantly and closely supervised or counseled. Could this constitute unlawful harassment or some form of discrimination? It could. What we hear in this description is at least a perceived difference in treatment that may be based on the employee's membership in a protected class; i.e., his sex.

In 2017 the U.S. EEOC kept open for public comment "Proposed Harassment Enforcement Guidance." Topics covered included:

1. Covered bases and causation.
2. Harassment resulting in discrimination with respect to a term, condition, or privilege of employment.
3. Liability.
4. Systemic harassment.
5. Promising practices (my personal favorite).

Keep Yourself (and Your Company) Safe

Courts are not unanimous in their interpretation of whether an individual manager or supervisor may be held liable under Title VII of the Civil Rights Act for unlawful harassment or discrimination. So to be safe, presume you can be. And, because you may be given certain power and authority by the company to run business operations, including directing the work of employees, it is also likely that you are acting as an agent of the employer and can create legal liability not only for yourself but for the company by what you say, do, or fail to do. Your actions and your knowledge, and what you see, hear, and know, may be implied to be actions or knowledge of the company. So if you see or hear something that could be a violation of the law, you should tell your HR representative or, if you are the HR representative, begin an investigation.

Remember, too, that investigations can be very informal processes. An investigation is just a process by which you try to get to the truth of the matter. For example, an employee comes into your office and says he heard from Coworker A that Coworker B is feeling harassed by the courier who delivers mail each day. How do you investigate? It may be as simple as going to Coworker B and asking if everything is OK and if there is anything or anyone in the work environment, including any third party, which is making him uncomfortable. What is likely the first question Coworker B will ask you? "Who told you that?" Must you disclose your source? No. You may simply tell Coworker B that is not important and remind him that you do not know this for a fact. It was just brought to your attention as a possibility and you wanted to check and understand what was happening and ensure everything is OK. This can also be a great opportunity to remind the employee about your company's anti-harassment policy, the no-retaliation provision, and what resources he may use to report any concerns he may have.

So when it comes to conduct that is at least unprofessional, mean, rude, unkind, derogatory, etc., how do we determine whether that conduct also constitutes some form of unlawful harassment? The EEOC guidance referenced above addresses in the Introduction how to evaluate whether harassment violates federal EEO law, and on the three components of a hostile work environment:

1. Covered bases and causation

Was the conduct based on the protected status of the complainant? The guidance explains that the harassing conduct must be "because of" the covered basis. While not all courts agree, the EEOC notes that covered bases include sexual orientation, gender identity, transgender status, or intention to transition. This is in addition to other covered bases under a variety of federal laws the EEOC's is charged to enforce including age, race, color, religion, national origin, sex, and pregnancy. Of course other federal agencies are charged with enforcing other employment laws that include anti-harassment provisions on other covered bases such as military status and citizenship. And harassment that is based on a person's protected characteristic is covered even if the harasser is a member of the same protected class. As for causation, the protected status need not be the sole reason for the harassment. It is a reason then the conduct may be unlawful. Causation may be at least inferred by the context in which the behavior occurs; the timing of when it occurs; and/or comparative evidence that indicates a difference in treatment that might show protected status is more likely than not a factor in the behavior complained of.

2. Hostile work environment threshold

Was the conduct sufficiently severe or pervasive to create a hostile work environment? Here the EEOC considers (this means you should too): Was the conduct sufficiently severe or pervasive to create a hostile work environment? Was it both subjectively and objectively hostile? What conduct is part of the hostile work environment claim? What if some of the conduct was not directed at the complainant or occurred outside the workplace? The guidance reminds as, like the EEOC's website, that our EEO laws, "do not impose a general civility code that covers 'run-of the mill boorish, juvenile, or annoying behavior.' " But they should consider factors such as frequency and severity of the conduct; whether it was physically threatening or humiliating; whether it unreasonably interfered with an employee's work performance; and whether it caused psychological harm. Some important things to remember and to remind all managers and supervisors may be related to where and to whom offensive must occur or be directed to constitute unlawful harassment. For example, conduct may occur outside of the complainant's presence as long as the complainant becomes aware of the conduct during his or her employment and it is sufficiently related to the complainant's work environment. So managers and supervisors take heed; once again monitor the workplace. You know that gossip, speculation, rumor mill in which people partake behind a coworker's back? Nip it in the bud. Quickly and firmly provide gentle reminders to "cut it out." Not only is it unkind and uncivil but it may also constitute unlawful harassment if based on a protected status. And what about conduct that occurs outside of the workplace? Can that constitute unlawful harassment? You bet! How, you ask? If employees threaten a coworker outside of work based on the coworker's protected status the mere presence of those same coworkers in the workplace can result in a hostile work environment for the employee that was threatened outside of work. And who has not yet encountered some issues with social media (raise your hand higher; I can't see you)? Let's say an employee is the subject of a racist comment that a coworker posts on social media, and other coworkers see the comment and discuss it at work, then the social media posting can contribute to a racially hostile work environment. And if managers are not yet convinced, the guidance notes, supervisor harassment that occurs outside the workplace is more likely to contribute to a hostile work environment than similar conduct by coworkers, given a supervisor's ability to affect a subordinate's employment status.

3. Liability

Is there a basis for holding the employer liable for the hostile work environment? The EEOC considers a combination of factors to determine whether the employer is liable including who the harasser is and whether the employee who was harassed was subjected to any tangible, adverse employment action (demotion, failure to promote, termination). You can see from Table 5.1 below that there really is no scenario where the employer could not be held liable. Where the employer may be liable, an opportunity may exist to either put forward an affirmative defense. In the case of an allegation of harassment by a supervisor the employer may show that it took reasonable care to prevent and correct the harassment from happening. Where the allegation of harassment involves a coworker the employer would need to show it was not negligent in preventing or correcting the harassment.

Table 5.1

	Harasser is Proxy of ER	Harasser is Supervisor	Harasser is Coworker
There is tangible adverse employment action	Strictly Liable	Strictly Liable	May be liable
There is no tangible adverse employment action	Strictly Liable	May be liable	May be liable

In its section on Promising Practices, the guidance shares five core principles that the EEOC finds have generally proven effective in preventing and addressing harassment:
- Committed and engaged leadership.
- Consistent and demonstrated accountability.
- Strong and comprehensive harassment policies.
- Trusted and accessible complaint procedures.
- Regular, interactive training tailored to the audience and the organization.

Aligned with these principles is a checklist with a dozen or more promising practices under each. Just a few are provided here; some you would expect and some may offer a few surprises:

Leadership and Accountability — train staff, managers and supervisors how to prevent, recognize, and respond to objectionable behavior; conduct anonymous employee surveys on a regular basis to assess whether harassment is occurring or is perceived to be tolerated.

Comprehensive and Effective Harassment Policy — include a statement that employees are encouraged to respond to questions or to otherwise participate in investigations into alleged harassment; translate your policy into all languages commonly used by employees; and provide the policy to employees upon hire and during harassment trainings and post it centrally, including on the company's internal website.

Effective and Accessible Harassment Complaint System — a good system should include processes to ensure that alleged harassers are not prematurely presumed guilty or prematurely disciplined for harassment; use guidelines to weigh the credibility of all relevant parties, prepare a written report documenting the investigation, findings, recommendations, and disciplinary, corrective, and preventative action taken (if any). NOTE: Remember this is the EEOC's proposed recommendation. Talk to your company's legal counsel for tips on who should prepare this documentation, to whom it should be given, and where and how it should be retained.

Effective Harassment Training — Tailor your training to the specific workplace and workforce; have it conducted by qualified, live, interactive trainers or, if live training is not feasible, designed to include active engagement by participants; and provide managers and supervisors with additional training that addresses their duties and responsibilities. The guidance suggests employers might also provide new forms of training, such as *workplace civility training* and/or bystander intervention training, to prevent workplace harassment

Workplace Bullying

The Workplace Bullying Institute conducts a national survey periodically to assess workplace bullying. In early 2014 Zogby Analytics was commissioned by the Workplace Bullying Institute to conduct an online survey of 1,000 adults in the U.S.[6] For purposes of the survey, workplace bullying was defined as repeated mistreatment; abusive conduct that is threatening, humiliating, or intimidating; work sabotage; or verbal abuse. The survey looks at this issue from a variety of angles from the parties' race, gender, rank (relationship to one another such as coworker, supervisor, or direct report), and more. Here are some of the results from the 2014 survey that you may find of interest (visit the websites listed in the endnotes to download a free, full copy of the survey).

- 27 percent of the respondents indicated that they are currently or within the last year have been a victim of workplace bullying (7 percent) or have been a victim of workplace bullying at some time prior to that (20 percent).

- When it comes to the sex of the target or victim, women target women at a higher rate than men: 68 percent as compared to 57 percent.
- Non-whites report being a victim of or affected by workplace bullying at rates higher than whites.
- While more than half of the bullies are bosses (56 percent), 33 percent of the bullies are coworkers, leaving 11 percent of the bullies as direct reports (yes, that's right. The boss can be a victim, too).
- 38 percent of the coworkers who witnessed bullying reported doing nothing.
- 29 percent of the victims reported leaving their job to avoid further bullying.
- In the 2010 survey, 40 percent of those who felt that they were or had been bullied never reported it to their employer. That factor was not reported in the 2014 survey.[7]

Now consider this data in light of the EEOC's 2017 guidance referenced earlier suggesting that a "promising practice" for employers is to provide civility and bystander intervention training. This is just another example of why open communication is critical to maintaining positive employee relations. Reinforcement and support needs to come from peers and colleagues as well as supervisors and managers.

Workplace Retaliation

For at least seven years in a row, this was the most frequently cited basis all of charges filed with the U.S. EEOC (FY 2010-2016). It was tied with race at 36 percent in EEOC FY 2009. And those figures have essentially doubled since 1998. So it should be no surprise that on August 25, 2016, the EEOC published new Enforcement Guidance on Retaliation and Related Issues.[8] One goal of the Guidance was to "be useful for employers, employees, and practitioners seeking detailed information about the EEOC's position on retaliation issues, and for employers seeking promising practices." And the EEOC is not the only federal agency with its eye on this issue.

On May 12, 2016, OSHA included in its final rule on recordkeeping new anti-retaliation provisions.[9] What was the agency's goal? "Under the final rule, OSHA will be able to cite an employer for retaliation even if the employee did not file a complaint, or if the employer has a program that deters or discourages reporting through the threat of retaliation." Previously the agency could only do so if the employee filed a claim within 30 days of the alleged retaliatory action. The rule has three key provisions:

1. An employer's procedure for reporting work-related injuries and illnesses must be reasonable and must not deter or discourage employees from reporting.
2. Employers must inform employees of their right to report work-related injuries and illnesses free from retaliation.
3. An employer may not retaliate against employees for reporting work-related injuries or illnesses.

Wait, there's more. On December 20, 2016, four federal agencies jointly published a Fact Sheet called "Retaliation Based on Exercise of Workplace Rights Is Unlawful."[10] What was the purpose of this publication? "This fact sheet clarifies that retaliation against workers who assert workplace rights is unlawful, regardless of the workers' immigration status." The agencies then describe the respective statutes that they are empowered to enforce:

- The Department of Justice (the Immigration and Nationality Act).
- The Department of Labor (the Fair Labor Standards Act, the Occupational Safety and Health Act, and laws enforced by the Office of Federal Contract Compliance Programs prohibiting employment discrimination by federal contractors).
- The EEOC (all EEOC-enforced laws described earlier in this chapter).
- The National Labor Relations Board (the National Labor Relations Act).

When you have at least five federal agencies addressing workplace retaliation in a span of approximately seven months, I think that is called a clue. It is a hot topic on the radar of those agencies so employers should be proactive; follow their recommendations and rules.

Practical Tips

- When an employee tells you that he is being harassed, ask the employee to describe the behaviors or actions that are occurring. If they are being directed at the employee, ask the employee why he thinks he is the target of the behavior. Then listen. If the employee replies that he thinks it is because of his membership in a legally protected class such as the employee's age, race, religion, sex, nationality, disability, etc., consider it a report of unlawful harassment and then begin an investigation. If you do not hear any reference to membership in a protected class, do not ignore it; this could still signal an employee relations matter and you should take steps to facilitate and resolve the matter.
- "Reboot" your harassment prevention training as the EEOC suggests. Consider including training on civility, with behavioral examples and expectations for professional conduct (yes, even at company parties and off-site events). Include information on bystander intervention, what resources coworkers have to report bullying or harassment of others, and their right to be free from retaliation as a result.
- I shared this tip in the previous chapter and feel compelled to do so again here. If your company has employment practices liability insurance (EPLI), check with your carrier to determine if it will give your company a discount if you have conducted or will conduct regular, periodic harassment training, have specific anti-harassment policies in your company's employee handbook, and/or conduct an HR compliance audit. If your company does not carry EPLI coverage, you may want to contact several insurance carriers to get several quotes to compare.
- Again, as the EEOC suggests, offer supplemental or additional training for your managers. You can save time and money by providing combined training programs with managers and staff

together for your core content. Then provide additional information for your supervisors and managers reinforcing their obligation and duty to prevent and correct unlawful harassment as well as the potential for individual liability and creating corporate liability should they fail to do so.

- In all of the above, ensure you are clearly communicating to all employees about their right to be free from retaliation. Ensure they understand that the right applies whether they are the person who expresses the concern or a witness who participates in a related investigation.

6

What's in a Name? Properly Classifying Your Workers

We classify our workers in a number of ways. First, we consider whether the worker is an employee or if the person falls under some other type of working relationship (volunteer, unpaid intern, independent contractor). Once we determine that the worker is an employee, we need also to determine whether the employee qualifies for exempt status or must be classified as non-exempt under the Fair Labor Standards Act (FLSA) and state regulations where applicable. In addition, what will be the nature of the employment relationship? Will it be at-will, contractual, a combination of the two (as they are not necessarily mutually exclusive), or something else? This chapter addresses some key concepts in each of these areas.

Plenty of people perform work for your company. But not every worker is necessarily an employee. You may have vendors, independent contractors, other contractors, subcontractors, agency temps, leased workers from a professional employer organization (PEO), volunteers, interns, and more. So let's consider some of these.

Independent Contractors

On July 24, 2007, I had the distinct honor of testifying on behalf of SHRM before the Subcommittee on Health, Employment, Labor and Pensions and the Workforce Protections Committee on Education and Labor in the U.S. House of Representatives during a joint hearing on the "Misclassification of Workers as Independent Contractors: What Policies and Practices Best Protect Workers?" Fast forward nearly a decade. President Obama's budget request before leaving office and for 2017 included $10 million in funding to revive a DOL grant program to help states combat worker misclassification.[1]

Why? Every new working relationship brings with it the challenge of asking the right questions to ensure that the employee is being properly classified as an employee or non-employee worker. And much of the difficulty lies with the fact that there is not a single definition of an employee; rather, there are numerous definitions and statutes that apply depending on the context in which you are asking the question. In 1992, even the U.S. Supreme Court held that there is "no definition that solves all problems as to the limitations of the employer-employee relationship." The Court explained that where a statute contains a term such as "employee" and does not "helpfully define it, this Court presumes that Congress means an agency law definition unless it clearly indicates otherwise." For example, the Court looked at the definition of employee in the Employee Retirement Income Security Act or ERISA and found the definition of employee "is completely circular and explains nothing."

For another example, look at Section 825.105 of the FMLA regulations that reads, in part, "The courts have said that there is no definition that solves all problems as to the limitations of the employer-employee relationship under the Act; and that determination of the relation cannot be based on "isolated factors" or upon a single characteristic or "technical concepts," but depends "upon the circumstances of the whole activity" including the underlying "economic reality."

And in 2003 the U.S. Supreme Court, in a separate decision, citing guidance from the U.S. Equal Employment Opportunity Commission, used a different test when trying to assess whether a managing partner of a firm (physician practice) should be counted as an employee under the Americans with Disabilities Act.

From federal statutes to agency guidance from the Internal Revenue Service (IRS) to state laws including workers' compensation and unemployment insurance, they all vary. Here's just one real-life example. A small business owner had only about ten employees. This business provides audio-visual support services. Of his ten employees, he has just one sound engineer. The engineer is highly skilled, quick and remarkably adept at assessing a problem and fixing it. He is a highly valued employee.

One day that employee tells the business owner that he wants to start his own business specializing in sound engineering only. They agree this would not be direct competition. The employee needs significant periods of time off from work to begin marketing and setting up his new business. The employer's policies do not provide for the kind of time off that this employee wants. The employee then offers that in lieu of resigning, he would be willing to be available on an as-needed basis and would work as an independent contractor and receive a 1099 form. The employer is delighted to be able retain access to this employee's skills and agrees.

They then agree to a part-time on-call work schedule and agree that the (former) employee may continue to use and have access to company equipment and will be paid on the same basis but as an independent contractor. Both parties are delighted to have worked out an arrangement that is amenable to both. That is, until the business owner is advised by legal counsel (yeah, that's me — the bearer of bad news) as to the possible pitfalls of proceeding. He now has to decide whether to risk a possible determination that he may have misclassified this employee in order to keep this highly skilled worker or to take no risk but end up losing the employee altogether, leaving neither of them happy. As of this writing, at least 21 states and the District of Columbia have passed laws, issued executive orders, or considered legislation addressing the improper classification of employees as independent contractors. Another 37 states have signed a memorandum of understanding (MOU) with the Department of Labor and the Internal Revenue Service agreeing to share state tax and payroll records for the purpose of finding workers who have been misclassified as independent contractors instead of employees.[2]

So where do you begin to assess the nature of the employment relationship? I find that question difficult to answer. It has been my experience that where a state law or regulation exists, it is usually stricter than federal definitions. So you might start there. Then, consider at least the DOL and IRS interpretation and guidance.

In May 2014 the DOL published an updated "Fact Sheet 13: Am I an Employee?: Employment Relationship Under the Fair Labor Standards Act (FLSA)."[3] Fourteen months later, on July 15, 2015, the DOL published an Administrator's Interpretation (AI), "The Application of the Fair Labor Standards Act's 'Suffer or Permit' Standard in the Identification of Employees Who Are Misclassified as Independent Contractors."[4] In short, the 15 pages describe a significant shift away from the amount of control an employer exerts with regard to where, when and how a worker performs the duties of a job. "All of the factors must be considered in each case, and no one factor (particularly the control factor) is determinative of whether a worker is an employee … The 'control' factor, for example, should not be given undue weight." The AI lays out the factors to consider under the economic realities test as a guide to determine whether a worker is really an employee or an independent contractor.

1. Is the work an integral part of the employer's business?
2. Does the worker's managerial skill affect the worker's opportunity for profit or loss?
3. How does the worker's relative investment compare to the employer's investment?
4. Does the work performed require special skill and initiative?
5. Is the relationship between the worker and the employer permanent or indefinite?
6. What is the nature and degree of the employer's control?

And how should an employer apply these factors? Are they weighted evenly? Must all, most or just some be met? The AI explains, "Ultimately, the goal is not simply to tally which factors are met, but to determine whether the worker is economically dependent on the employer (and thus its employee) or is really in business for him or herself (and thus its independent contractor). The factors are a guide to make this ultimate determination of economic dependence or independence.

Next you might turn to the IRS guidance found in publication 1779.[5] As if speaking to the worker, the publication reads in part:

- Behavioral Control
  - › Instructions — if you receive extensive instructions on how work is to be done, this suggests that you are an employee.
  - › Training — if the business provides you with training about required procedures and methods, this indicates that the business wants the work done in a certain way, and this suggests that you may be an employee.
- Financial Control
  - › Significant Investment — if you have a significant investment in your work, you may be an independent contractor.
  - › Expenses — if you are not reimbursed for some or all business expenses, then you may be an independent contractor.
  - › Opportunity for Profit or Loss — if you can realize a profit or incur a loss, this suggests that you are in business for yourself and that you may be an independent contractor.
- Relationship of the Parties
  - › Employee Benefits — if you receive benefits, such as insurance, pension, or paid leave, this is an indication that you may be an employee.
  - › Written Contracts — a written contract may show what both you and the business intend.

How are these factors weighed? Generally, if you end up with a tie between financial and behavioral control then a written document that shows the intent of the parties might be the tie breaker. The IRS publication reads, with regard to the relationship of the parties factor, "This may be very significant if it is difficult, if not impossible, to determine status based on other facts."

If your worker passes the above tests, it would seem you may properly classify your worker as an independent contractor. But proceed with caution; as with so many issues, consult with your company's employment counsel. Misclassifying workers can have serious adverse consequences for your company related to workers' compensation coverage, ERISA liability, union organizing drives, Family and Medical Leave Act (FMLA) coverage, tax liability, and so much more.

Interns and Volunteers

Throughout the year many employers contemplate having interns — usually students, retired persons, or displaced workers seeking to remain active in the workforce — perform work for them during the summer months, holidays, or seasonal periods when the volume of business increases. A common question is if and when these individuals must be paid and how much. Unpaid internships are permitted under the Fair Labor Standards Act (FLSA) and the DOL has published a related Fact Sheet[6] and employers should ensure that their intern(s) meet all of the following factors:

1. The internship, even though it includes actual operation of the facilities of the employer, is similar to training that would be given in an educational environment;
2. The internship experience is for the benefit of the intern;
3. The intern does not displace regular employees but works under close supervision of existing staff;
4. The employer that provides the training derives no immediate advantage from the activities of the intern and, on occasion, its operations may actually be impeded;
5. The intern is not necessarily entitled to a job at the conclusion of the internship; and
6. The employer and the intern understand that the intern is not entitled to wages for the time spent in the internship.

Notice the "and" between factors 5 and 6. This test, if you will, is unlike some of the tests used to determine employee versus independent contractor status that are weighed. All six factors must be met. If any one factor is not met, it is unlikely the person can be properly classified as an unpaid intern. For example, let's say your company recently had a reduction in force (RIF) and placed a temporary freeze on hiring any new employees. Simultaneously, you have a lot going on; your company is changing its payroll and HRIS systems. You are also a government contractor, and it is time for you to update your written affirmative action plans. With so much on your plate, you do not have time to get these tasks done but you cannot hire someone to help you, even on a part-time, temporary basis. So you think about contacting a local college to find an intern to do this work for free. Would these assignments qualify for an unpaid internship?

Apply the questions above. Factors 1 and 3 may not be met. The training related to updating affirmative action plans may not be like that provided in an academic environment. And while the intern may work under close supervision, is he not actually displacing another worker? You are seeking an intern because you cannot hire. If you did not have the hiring freeze, you might actually hire a temporary, part-time employee to do this work. If that is the case, then you may not meet this factor No. 3 either. Thus, using someone in this role as an unpaid intern may not be proper. On the other hand, if your company is providing job shadowing opportunities that allow an intern to learn certain functions under the close and constant supervision of regular employees, but the intern performs no or minimal work, the activity is more likely to be viewed as a bona fide education experience. So what is the remedy? In this scenario, there may not be one since there is a hiring freeze. In another instance, the company could simply bring the student intern on and pay him minimum wage (of course the higher of federal or state) for the time worked. The DOL also notes that unpaid internships in the public sector and for non-profit charitable organizations, where the intern volunteers without expectation of compensation, are generally permissible.

And what about volunteers? As the economy changes, many people seek new ways of networking to find employment opportunities: Young workers may be drawn to volunteer roles to gain practical work experience that may lead to employment; older workers who have retired may volunteer their time to businesses so they may continue to serve the local community; and individuals in transition may want to volunteer to keep their skills and knowledge current. Whatever the individual's motivation, the employer needs to ensure that these individuals properly qualify for unpaid volunteer status. The DOL Field Operations Handbook dated September 21, 2016, provides in Section 64c04 that volunteers usually do so on a part-time basis, have no expectation of remuneration or employment and support non-profit organizations. What about for-profit entities? The handbook directs DOL field personnel, "If questions arise about the use of volunteers by for-profit organizations or employers, contact the NO, OP, DEPP, FMLA/OLS Branch." The acronyms refer to National Office (NO), Office of Policy (OP), Division of Enforcement Policy and Procedures (DEPP), and Family and Medical Leave Act and Other Labor Standards (FMLA/OLS) Branch. Thus, a volunteer who sits with babies in the neo-natal intensive care unit of a local hospital, who volunteers his time to walk dogs at the local animal shelter, or who donates his time to help at a local soup kitchen, may qualify for volunteer status. As with other worker classification decisions, take care to ensure that the classification you apply is correct.

The Basic Nature of the Employment Relationship

Now that you have determined that a worker is, in fact, your employee, what will define the nature of that employment relationship?

At-Will Employment

Currently, 49 of our 50 states are at-will employment states. Generally, employment at-will means the employment relationship will only continue at the will of both parties; that is, employment may be terminated by either party (the employee or employer), at any time, for any reason or no reason, with or without notice. As of this writing, Montana is the exception and has a law that permits employers only to discharge an employee for "good cause," except during the employee's probationary period. If the employer does not define a probationary period, then that period is presumed to be six months.[7]

The nature of the at-will employment relationship, however, does not permit an employer to take adverse employment action (discharge, demotion, corrective action, etc.) for unlawful reasons. The latter could include action based upon an employee's actual or perceived membership in a legally protected class such as age, race, religion, sex, nationality, disability, etc. The same may apply to the status of an individual with whom an employee associates. Chapter 3 helps explain why an employer should take the time to retain its employees despite the fact that the employment relationship continues only at the will of both parties.

Contractual Employment

Some employers use employment contracts for certain newly hired employees; some may use them for executives; some may use them for sales staff that incorporate a non-compete and/or no-solicitation agreement; and some may use them to simply spell out the expectations of the relationship. Whatever the reason, intent, or purpose contractual employment does not have to be mutually exclusive of at-will employment. It is very possible to have a contract with one of your employees that also clarifies that the employment relationship is at-will and can be terminated by either party at any time.

Collective Bargaining Agreements

These create an employment relationship that is generally not at-will. Collective bargaining agreements (CBAs) commonly provide that members of the union or those represented by the union may not be terminated from employment without "just cause." That is, the employer must provide a reason for the termination, such as excessive absenteeism, lateness, poor work performance, etc. The CBA may then spell out what steps the employer must follow before taking any adverse action and what rights the employee has upon receipt of such action, such as filing a grievance or compelling arbitration. If you started this book from the beginning, which is the end of the employment relationship, you read the pre-termination checklist. Those considerations — known as the elements of just cause — are actually regularly used by arbitrators in the collective bargaining arena. While I have found that those elements vary in number and description from author to author, the five elements I have described in Chapter 1 are those I have found to be generally common. That is why I find them to be a great, proactive guide when considering terminating the employment of any employee, union or non-union.

FLSA Status

A step that may be subsequent to determining the nature of the working relationship and that it will, in fact, be an employment relationship is assessing whether the employee qualifies for exempt status under the FLSA. The DOL starts from the presumption that every employee is non-exempt, that is, the employee must be paid on an hourly basis, earn at least minimum wage (federal or state, whichever is higher), and one and one-half times the employee's regular rate of pay for each hour worked over 40 in any workweek. You, the employer, have the burden to show that any employee qualifies for exempt classification. In order to establish that qualification, you must bear the burden of proof and demonstrate that three key elements or "tests" under the federal regulations have been met. The employee must:

1. Be paid a guaranteed minimum salary established by the DOL.
2. Be paid that guaranteed minimum salary on a salary basis.
3. Meet one of three primary duties tests.

Some Background

The FLSA was passed in 1938. The minimum salary threshold was increased seven times between 1938 and 2004. On March 13, 2014, President Barack Obama directed the DOL to "modernize and streamline" the FLSA overtime regulations. On June 30, 2015, the DOL announced proposed changes to the section 541 FLSA regulations governing overtime determination and coverage. Then the fascinating chain of events began.

- On May 18, 2016, the DOL released its final regulations making changes to the overtime exemptions.
- On June 23, 2016, I had the honor of testifying before the U.S. House Small Business Committee hearing on "Damaging Repercussions: DOL's Overtime Rule, Small Employers and their Employees." The final rule was to take effect December 1, 2016.

- Just days before, on November 22, 2016, the judge for the U.S. District Court for the Eastern District of Texas issued a preliminary injunction effectively blocking implementation of the rule.
- On February 16, 2017, I again had the honor to return to Congress and testify on behalf of SHRM. This time it was before the U.S. House Committee on Education and the Workforce Subcommittee on Workforce Protections hearing on "Federal Wage and Hour Policies in the Twenty-First Century Economy."
- On February 22, 2017, a federal appeals court granted the DOL a second extension to May 1, 2017 to determine what its position would be on the final overtime rule in light of the change in the administration following President Donald Trump's election.
- Then in April 2017 the DOL was granted yet another extension through June 30, 2017.
- That's where we are as of this writing. So regardless of where this lands and whatever the new minimum salary threshold will be, the general platform for applying it will likely remain the same. So let's start with the minimum salary test.

Minimum Salary Test

Whatever the level is, this is probably the easiest of the three tests to apply. If the employee is not paid at least the guaranteed minimum salary established by the DOL, you need not even bother with the other two tests. That employee must be classified as non-exempt. OK, it is almost as easy as that. Here are some common questions related to the minimum salary test:

Q: The minimum salary test is usually described as a minimum weekly as well as an annual salary. Does it matter which we use so long as the employee meets one or the other?

A: Yes, it does matter. The employee must be paid at least the weekly minimum salary. For example, an employee might have a minimum weekly salary that varies and we know moving forward that some weeks he will be paid at a level that is below the weekly threshold. Even if by the end of the year the employee's total base salary met the annual minimum he would not have met the minimum weekly salary.

Q: Are there any exceptions or any jobs to which the minimum salary does not apply?
A: Yes. The minimum salary test does not apply to certain teachers, computer employees, employees who hold a valid license or certificate permitting, and who are actually engaged in, the practice of law or medicine with a number of exceptions; and to employees who hold the requisite academic degree for the general practice of medicine and are engaged in an internship or resident program pursuant to the practice of the profession.

Q: Can we prorate the guaranteed minimum salary so a part-time employee will meet the minimum salary test?
A: No. The minimum salary test applies to the employee, not to the job. If that employee does not earn at least the minimum weekly salary, he must be classified as non-exempt.

Salary Basis Test

The employee must be paid his guaranteed minimum salary not subject to reduction because of variations in the quality or quantity of the work performed.[8] There are seven exceptions to this rule under the federal regulations:

1. Deductions from pay may be made when an exempt employee is absent from work for one or more full days for personal reasons, other than sickness or disability.

2. Deductions from pay may be made for absences of one or more full days occasioned by sickness or disability (including work-related accidents) if the deduction is made in accordance with a bona fide plan, policy, or practice of providing compensation for loss of salary occasioned by such sickness or disability.

3. While an employer cannot make deductions from pay for absences of an exempt employee occasioned by jury duty, attendance as a

witness, or temporary military leave, the employer can offset any amounts received by an employee as jury fees, witness fees, or military pay for a particular week against the salary due for that particular week without loss of the exemption.

4. Deductions from pay of exempt employees may be made for penalties imposed in good faith for infractions of safety rules of major significance.

5. Deductions from pay of exempt employees may be made for unpaid disciplinary suspensions of one or more full days imposed in good faith for infractions of workplace conduct rules. Such suspensions must be imposed pursuant to a written policy applicable to all employees.

6. An employer is not required to pay the full salary in the initial or terminal week of employment. Rather, an employer may pay a proportionate part of an employee's full salary for the time actually worked in the first and last week of employment.

7. An employer is not required to pay the full salary for weeks in which an exempt employee takes unpaid leave under the FMLA. Rather, when an exempt employee takes unpaid leave under the FMLA, an employer may pay a proportionate part of the full salary for time actually worked.

Each winter, questions also arise as to whether an employer may require exempt employees to use paid leave and/or make deductions from exempt employees' wages for full- or partial-day absences due to inclement weather. The DOL has issued a number of opinion letters on this matter.[9] The general answer is that employers may require an exempt employee to use paid leave for such absences. If the exempt employee has exhausted all paid leave, then the employer may deduct from the exempt employee's wage for a full-day absence but generally not a partial-day of absence.

Another common question is with regard to making deductions from an exempt employee's wages for lost or damaged company property. For example, let's say a company issues an identification badge to all employees. The company has a policy that if an employee loses or damages his ID badge, a $15 fee will be deducted from the employee's wage to replace the badge. According to a DOL opinion letter, that policy defeats the salary basis of payment for an exempt employee.[10] What if the employer did not deduct the replacement fee from the exempt employee's wage but required him to pay the fee directly to the employer? The DOL opinion letter indicates that this is effectively the same as a deduction and would also violate the salary basis of payment.

Duties Tests: Executive, Administrative, and Professional Exemptions

Executive Exemption

- In order to qualify for exempt status under the executive exemption, an employee must meet each of the following tests: The employee's primary duty must be managing the enterprise, or managing a customarily recognized department or subdivision of the enterprise;
- The employee must customarily and regularly direct the work of at least two or more other full-time employees or their equivalent; and
- The employee must have the authority to hire or fire other employees, or the employee's suggestions and recommendations as to the hiring, firing, advancement, promotion, or any other change of status of other employees must be given particular weight.[11]

Employers often get tripped up in this category when a team leader, supervisor, or manager performs both exempt and non-exempt duties.

A supervisor who has the authority to hire and fire and who regularly supervises two or more full-time equivalents (FTEs), but who also performs non-exempt duties, must have as his primary duty the performance of the exempt duties. While primary work is often assessed by the amount of time an employee spends on it, that is not the only factor. Primary duty means the principal, main, major, or most important duty that the employee performs. Determination of an employee's primary duty must be based on all the facts in a particular case, with the major emphasis on the character of the employee's job as a whole.

Administrative Exemption

In order to qualify for exempt status under the administrative exemption, an employee must meet each of the following tests:

- The employee's primary duty must be the performance of office or non-manual work directly related to the management or general business operations of the employer or the employer's customers; and
- The employee's primary duty includes the exercise of discretion and independent judgment with respect to matters of significance.[12]

This title can be misleading. You may read the word "administrative" and think that it refers to administrative assistants (AAs). While an AA may be properly classified as exempt, this exemption refers to an individual who administers business operations such as developing and implementing marketing plans and programs, developing and administering human resource policies, and engaging in contract negotiations with vendors and contractors as just a few examples. Having the authority to independently exercise discretion and control over these activities is a critical component to qualifying for this exemption.

Professional Exemption

In order to qualify for exempt status under the professional exemption, an employee must meet each of the following tests:

- The employee's primary duty must be the performance of work requiring advanced knowledge, defined as work that is predominantly intellectual in character and that includes the consistent exercise of discretion and judgment;
- The advanced knowledge must be in a field of science or learning; and
- The advanced knowledge must be customarily acquired by a prolonged course of specialized intellectual instruction.[13]

A key here is to remember that the job requires the advanced degree and not just that the individual *has* the advanced degree. For example, if a librarian has a master's in library science degree but the job he holds does not *require* that degree, then he may not qualify for the professional exemption. The employee may, however, qualify for exempt status under the executive or administrative exemption.

Remember that the above analyses must be conducted for each employee, not just by job classification. For example, you might have five incumbents in the same job classification who all meet the duties test and are paid on a salary basis. But if one is a part-time employee and earns less than $455 per week, that individual would have to be classified as non-exempt. Or perhaps all five are paid on a salary basis and meet the minimum salary test but one is a sub-par performer and, while the job requires the exercise of discretion and independent judgment, this one employee is not fulfilling those duties. That employee may have to be classified as non-exempt.

There are a number of states that have their own executive, administrative and professional (EAP) regulations that define these exempt classifications differently from the federal regulations. When the final rule did not take effect as scheduled on December 1, 2016, some states responded by considering legislation that would implement similar regulations at the state level. This trend may continue until the matter is resolved at the federal level. If you have business operations in any of these states, then you will need to conduct a dual analysis and repeat this process following the regulations in your state(s). Also be sure that any wage deductions you make are also in accordance with the wage and hour laws of the state(s) in which you do business. Many states have laws that prohibit certain deductions that are otherwise permissible under federal law.

Practical Tips

- Just because employment is at-will does not mean you have no liability when terminating the employment relationship. Let bona fide business needs, not emotion, drive your employment decisions.
- When in doubt, classify conservatively:
  › If you conduct an FLSA analysis and are still not sure whether a position fully qualifies for exempt status, then classify the position as non-exempt.

> › If you conduct a classification analysis and are still not sure whether a worker will be an employee or independent contractor, then classify the worker as an employee.

- If you use unpaid student interns or volunteers, be sure they meet the "tests" described in this chapter. If not, or if you are unsure, then classify them as employees and pay them at least minimum wage.

- Be sure the terms of any employment contract provide you with the flexibility you want or need and do not obligate you to terms or conditions of employment that you did not intend.

7

Employee Handbooks: Read 'Em and Weep?

Like performance appraisals, all too often an employee handbook is used by a plaintiff to demonstrate or establish that his employer created an implied or express contract or created some obligation it did not otherwise intend. This chapter is intended only as a general guide for some proactive practices to consider when creating or updating your company's employee handbook. Remember to always consult with your company's legal counsel to ensure that your policies, practices, and procedures comply with the federal, state, and local laws and regulations in your states of operation.

A common first question is, *"Should we have an employee handbook?"* or *"Must we have an employee handbook?"* Under federal law, there is no requirement that an employer have an employee handbook. It is up to you. There are, however, advantages and disadvantages of having one. Advantages include:

1. Introducing employees to your company and its goals, mission, and expectations; using the handbook as an opportunity to brag about your company and share its history;
2. Providing clarification for your employees as to their benefits and your expectations; and
3. Helping to ensure consistency in providing benefits like paid leave, and guidance on when you will/will not provide training opportunities, promote from within or provide coaching, counseling, and correcting.

Disadvantages of employee handbooks generally arise only when handbooks are not drafted well. Examples may include when an employer unintentionally creates an implied contract or defeats the at-will employment relationship. We will consider some examples later in this chapter.

A next common question is, *"What should we include in our employee handbook?"* A challenge in creating a useful employee handbook is creating one that provides your employees with enough information to know what is expected of them and what they can expect from your company while not including so much information that the handbook becomes so lengthy that no one will read it. You also want to avoid including so much detail that you lose some of your discretion in making management decisions. At the end of this chapter, I have enclosed a sample table of contents as a general guide for some policies that seem to be common among many employers (see Table 7.1 at the end of the chapter). Some, of course, may not be applicable to your company, such as FMLA requirements that generally do not apply to employers with fewer than 50 employees. You should have an employment attorney review your employee handbook, whether it is your first or an updated version, to ensure it is compliant with the federal, state, and local laws and regulations that are applicable to your company. There are companies and vendors that offer or sell template employee handbooks as well as employment applications. That is fine and certainly can save you a lot of up-front work. It is likely, however, that the template will need to be tailored to not just meet your company's procedures, policies, and practices but to also comply with the laws and regulations of your state and local jurisdictions.

So now that we have answered two common threshold questions, let's address some proactive practices and pitfalls to avoid for some of the more common policies.

EEO & Anti-Harassment Policy Tips

Most if not all employee handbooks have equal employment opportunity (EEO) and anti-harassment policies. That's great, but what is important is what a proactive EEO policy actually includes. Most list a number of protected classes and might read, "We do not tolerate any form of unlawful discrimination and provide equal employment opportunities without regard to an individual's age, race, religion, color, sex, national origin, or disability." That statement addresses key protected classes covered under federal law, but not all, such as citizenship, genetic information, or military status. And there may be additional protected classes under your state or local laws. Since these protections change through the legislative process and would require you to rewrite your handbook every time a new federal, state, or local law is passed, you might include a caveat at the end of the sentence that reads, "... or on any other legally protected basis under federal, state, or local law." That lets the reader know that you know you have not listed all protected classes.

It may also be a proactive practice to include perception and association clauses in your EEO policy. Remember that Title VII of the Civil Rights Act of 1964 as well as the Americans with Disabilities Act (ADA) prohibit discrimination, which includes unlawful harassment based on the perception of an individual's membership in a protected class as well as the legally protected status of an individual with whom the individual associates.

What about your harassment policy? The EEOC's guidance published in 2016 recommends that a policy generally include:

- A clear explanation of prohibited conduct, including examples;
- Clear assurance that employees who make complaints or provide information related to complaints, witnesses, and others who participate in the investigation will be protected against retaliation;
- A clearly described complaint process that provides multiple, accessible avenues of complaint;
- Assurance that the employer will protect the confidentiality of harassment complaints to the extent possible;
- A complaint process that provides a prompt, thorough, and impartial investigation; and
- Assurance that the employer will take immediate and proportionate corrective action when it determines that harassment has occurred, and respond appropriately to behavior which may not be legally actionable "harassment" but which, left unchecked, may lead to same.

Employment Status Policy Tips

With some frequency, employee handbooks refer to full- and part-time employees but do not define these. In this case, an employee working anything less than 40 hours per week may be unsure if he is full- or part-time, such as if the employee works 35 hours per week. When defining full- and part-time, be sure to not leave a gap. For example, a policy might define full-time as being regularly scheduled to work at least 40 hours per week and part-time as regularly scheduled to work fewer than 35 hours per week. In this example, employees regularly scheduled to work at least 35 but less than 40 hours may be unclear as to whether they are full- or part-time employees.

Another proactive practice may be to use the term "regular" rather than "permanent" employees. The very nature of the at-will employment relationship, as well as many contractual employment relationships, is that employment is *not* permanent or guaranteed for any particular length of time or duration.

Now, remember the reference at the start of this chapter about how employee handbooks can create an unintended but enforceable implied contract? The probationary or introductory period policy is a great example. You may read in this type of policy that this period is "a time to put your best foot forward" and that the employer can let the employee go during this period, with or without notice or reason. So if you are a new employee and just read that policy, what might you think it implies? What impression do you have? Does it sound like something magical happens at the end of that introductory period? Does it sound like the employer might not be able to terminate you with or without notice or reason after this period? If you answered "Yes," some courts would agree.

Some courts have held that this type of language may create an implied contract because of the implication as described above. So should you have an introductory period policy? Ask yourself this, "Why do you want one?" How is the employment relationship during this period different from the day after this period? If there is no difference, then you probably do not want or need this policy. But if, for example, you do not permit employees in this period to accrue paid leave, or perhaps you allow them to accrue it but not use it, then use this policy to describe those differences.

Pay Issue Policy Tips

Many state laws require employers to give employees notice of their pay rate and payday upon hire. You may be able to meet this requirement by including that information in your employee handbook. Many pay issues are regulated by state laws and are too numerous to address here. A few pay issues that are commonly regulated at the state level include and are not limited to:

- *Pay at termination of wages and accrued, paid leave.* Some state laws require the payment of accrued paid leave at separation from employment under certain circumstances. And some state laws require you to issue the final paycheck within a certain period of time, depending upon whether the employee quit or was involuntarily terminated.

- *Pay frequency.* Some states require that employees, at least nonexempt ones, be paid at some interval more frequently than monthly, such as at least twice per month.

- *Payday that falls on a holiday or non-work day.* Some states require that if the payday falls on a holiday or other day that the employer is not open for business, then employees must be paid the immediately preceding work day. For example, a policy that provides that if the payday falls on a Sunday, then employees will be paid on Monday would not be permissible.

- *Direct deposit.* Some states limit or restrict an employer from requiring direct deposit.

- *Deductions from pay.* Some states prohibit certain deductions that may otherwise be permissible under the Fair Labor Standards Act (FLSA) such as for cash shortages, lost or damaged company property, negative paid leave bank balances, and more.

Common to most employers is the requirement under the FLSA that overtime be paid to non-exempt employees for all hours worked over 40 in a workweek. Keep in mind that your policy should read (and the law requires) that overtime is 1.5 times the employee's regular rate of pay, which may be different from the employee's hourly rate of pay. It may be proactive to use the phrase "regular" rate rather than "hourly" in your related policies. For example, if a non-exempt employee's hourly rate of pay is $10.00 and he receives a non-discretionary bonus of $100.00 for exceeding a particular performance or productivity goal in a one-month period, the value of the bonus may have to be calculated into the employee's hourly rate of pay for all hours worked in that month to determine his regular rate of pay for overtime calculations.

In addition, consider including the "safe harbor" policy provided by the Department of Labor (DOL). If an employer has a clearly communicated policy that prohibits improper pay deductions and includes a complaint mechanism, reimburses employees for any improper deductions, and makes a good-faith commitment to comply in the future, such employer will not lose the exemption for any employees unless the employer willfully violates the policy by continuing to make improper deductions after receiving employee complaints. The best evidence of a clearly communicated policy is having a written policy that was distributed to employees prior to the improper pay deductions by, for example, providing a copy of the policy to employees at the time of hire, publishing the policy in an employee handbook, or publishing the policy on the employer's Intranet.[1]

Why reinvent the wheel? The DOL has provided a sample "salary basis" policy that employers can use to incorporate into the company's employee handbook or related pay policies.[2]

Paid and Unpaid Leave

Aside from Family and Medical Leave Act (FMLA) leave for covered employers, there are myriad other forms of leave that employers may offer. Some are paid; some are not. We discussed the administrative considerations and some policy tips in Chapter 4. Aside from those, many employers offer some type of "personal" leave that may include time off for personal reasons or medical reasons that are not covered under FMLA. Once again, check the employment laws and regulations in your state(s) of operation to ensure these policies comply with any state requirements as well as your local jurisdictions. The latter have been actively enacting laws related to paid and unpaid leave. For example, some states may require certain employers to offer such leave, some may require that such leave be accompanied with pay, and some may require that such leave be available for the employee to care for an immediate family member as well as for the employee's own illness.

In addition, consider the following:

- Does your policy address whether "personal" leave is in addition to or runs concurrent with any other type of leave that you offer, such as paid leave?
- Does your policy let employees know whether they may or are required to exhaust any paid leave (vacation, sick, paid time off, or PTO) before being absent without pay?
- Does your policy include a maximum length of time that you may approve an unpaid leave of absence, such as six months, up to one year or the employee's length of employment, whichever is less?
- What does your policy say happens at the end of a leave period if the employee is unable to return to work? Does it read that the employee "will be" terminated? If so, consider replacing that with "may be" terminated. The EEOC suggests that "bright-line" leave policies may violate the ADA.
- Does your policy indicate for how long the employer will continue the employee on medical coverage, such as for 30 days or until the end of the month in which paid leave is exhausted?
- Does your policy include a notice indicating whether or not you will guarantee an employee reinstatement to the same position he had when he began the leave and, if not, what considerations you will offer, such as any comparable position for which he qualifies or any other position for which he qualifies?
- If you expect employees on leave to not apply for unemployment insurance benefits, does your policy expressly provide a notice to that effect and state what may happen if the employee does file for unemployment insurance (UI) benefits?

Professional Appearance

Dress code and appearance policies continue to make headlines as they may adversely impact employees based on race, religion, national origin, and more. Appearance includes everything from facial piercings to facial hair to attire, hair color, and more. Let's consider some current trends and information.

On November 18, 2016, the EEOC published updated guidance on national origin discrimination.[3] It reminds employers that, "A hostile work environment based on national origin can take different forms, including ethnic slurs, ridicule, intimidation, workplace graffiti, physical violence, or other offensive conduct directed toward an individual because of his birthplace, ethnicity, culture, language, dress, or foreign accent." Earlier guidance published by the EEOC provides, "For example, a dress code that prohibits certain kinds of ethnic dress, such as traditional African or East Indian attire, but otherwise permits casual dress would treat some employees less favorably because of their national origin.

"Moreover, if the dress code conflicts with an employee's religious practices and the employee requests an accommodation, the employer must modify the dress code or permit an exception to the dress code unless doing so would result in undue hardship.

"Similarly, if an employee requests an accommodation to the dress code because of his disability, the employer must modify the dress code or permit an exception to the dress code, unless doing so would result in undue hardship."[4]

The National Labor Relations Board's View

On March 18, 2015, the General Counsel's Office of the NLRB published Memorandum GC 15-04, Report of the General Counsel Concerning Employer Rules.[5] The memo covered a variety of topics generally addressed in employers' employee handbooks. The guidance gives examples of policy language that violates the National Labor Relations Act (NLRA), some that do not and why. Topics covered include:

- Confidentiality.
- Employee conduct toward the company and supervisors.
- Employee conduct toward fellow employees.
- Employee interaction with third parties.
- Use of company logo, copyright and trademarks.

- Photography and recording.
- Leaving work.
- Conflict of interest.

I dare say you may find some of the interpretations fascinating and challenging, particularly as they address conduct and (in)civility and employees' rights to access company materials and property that you might think are completely proprietary. While employers may see some of the restrictions as challenging, I do find the memo helpful in the respect that it provides the "why." It explains why the board feels certain policies violate the NLRA and would unduly "chill" or discourage employees from exercising their Section 7 rights, e.g., to act in concert for the purpose of collective bargaining or other mutual aid or protection. One practical example is employees' right to discuss their wages with one another.

Electronic Communications

A few years before publishing the memo described above, on May 30, 2012, the NLRB published the third of three memos on social media.[6] Again, it gave examples of employers' social media policies that violated the NLRA. This third memo also included a sample policy. Employers may want to consult their legal counsel to determine if that sample is still a good model today and should be used in a current employee handbook.

Practical Tips

- Policy versus practice. Remember that no matter how well your employee handbook is written, it is only as good as how well you apply and enforce it. If you rarely enforce any particular policy, the day you want to do so may likely be the day you give the appearance of adverse treatment based on an individual's protected status.
- Consistency. As has been mentioned throughout this book, this does not mean that you have to treat every employee in exactly the same way. You may make exceptions to the rule and treat employees equitably rather than equally. Be sure, however, you have a valid business reason for making an exception.

- Regular updates. Sometimes it might be better to have no employee handbook than an old or outdated one. There is no strict rule, but consider updating your handbook at least every 12 to 18 months. You will likely find that even if federal employment laws have not changed, there may be new federal or state regulations, new state or local laws, or case law that has modified the interpretations of existing laws.

Table 7.1

continued on next page

Table 7.1

8

Welcome Onboard!

It is your employee's first day of work, and you have already invested a lot of time and money to get him there, right? You advertised, reviewed resumes, interviewed candidates, and perhaps conducted some pre-employment assessments or post-offer medical exams or questionnaires. Now how do you begin to reap a reward and positive return on the investment (ROI) on all that time and money? What is the difference between new employee orientation (NEO) and onboarding? Is the latter just a different name for what employers have done for years or is it truly different? The answer is, of course, it depends. You can give the program you have for new employees most any name. The questions you should be asking are what is it, what is it intended to do, and what does it actually do?

I distinguish between the two (NEO and onboarding) as an event versus a process. New employee orientation is an event; onboarding is a process. Neither is right or wrong, good or bad; they are, however, different. Onboarding provides employees with an ongoing process by which they are acclimated to your company's mission, vision, philosophy, methodologies, business operations, procedures, and more. It is broader in scope and more in-depth.

SHRM published in conjunction with Right Management, "Onboarding New Employees: Maximizing Success."[1] It tells us, in part that, "Half of all hourly workers leave new jobs in the first four months, and half of senior outside hires fail within 18 months." There's the business case for developing and administering a program that welcomes, orients, and acclimates your new employees to your organization. The publication provides a list of recommended practices for onboarding:

- Implement the basics prior to the first day on the job.
- Make the first day on the job special.
- Use formal orientation programs.
- Develop a written onboarding plan.
- Make onboarding participatory.
- Be sure your program is consistently implemented.
- Ensure that the program is monitored over time.
- Use technology to facilitate the process.
- Use milestones, such as 30, 60, 90, and 120 days on the job — and up to one year post-organizational entry — to check in on employee progress.
- Engage stakeholders in planning.
- Include key stakeholder meetings as part of the program.
- Be crystal clear with new employees in terms of:
  › Objectives.
  › Timelines.
  › Roles.
  › Responsibilities

A 2015 article in *Forbes* cited a study published in the *Academy of Management Journal* that found that the first 90 days of employment is pivotal to building rapport with the company, management, and coworkers.[2] The article suggests that, among other things:

- Structured onboarding increases retention — According to a 2007 study by the Wynhurst Group, when employees go through structured onboarding, they are 58 percent more likely to remain with the organization after three years.
- Training must encompass how and why (this one is my personal favorite, "The Power of Why!") — According to a CareerBuilder report, 60 percent of employees feel that skills will be learned on the job, but 49 percent of employers feel that training is an equal responsibility of employees and employers.

- So with all this advice and so much more available to you, where do you begin? The program that is best for your organization depends upon many factors: your company size; how many employees you hire each month or week; your industry; what is important to you that employees know and understand; and so much more. A full-blown onboarding program may not be feasible for a smaller employer. But if you consider some of the basic elements, a modified version may be a great fit for most any employer.

Employment Engagement

Not convinced yet? The Gallup Organization reports the following:

- In 2013 only 13 percent of employees around the world were engaged at work.[3]
- In 2015 that figure still did not paint a pretty picture but looked better as 31.5 percent of U.S. employees were engaged.[4]
- 2016 saw little improvement with 32 percent of U.S. employees reported as engaged.[5]

What are some practical examples of activities included in onboarding programs? Some invite the new employee's immediate family members to visit the worksite (usually before the first day of work), have a guided tour, and meet the employee's new manager and HR representative in an effort to welcome them and help them feel a part of the new "community." This, of course, takes time and may not be feasible in all industries, particularly if the worksite is a contracted or government worksite or an otherwise secured facility. You could tailor this process to one that will work for you, your organization, and the new employee.

Day One

If your company is on the smaller size or hires just a few employees each month, then you may choose to orient new employees one-on-one rather than in a large group as part of a new employee orientation program. Larger employers may have monthly or semi-monthly NEO programs with 20 or more employees in the audience for each program. Whichever method you develop and use, be sure each employee's first day is interactive. The ideal is to actively engage the employee from at least Day One. Do not give the employee a copy of your employee handbook and that big, fat folder with all the new-hire paperwork and forms and have the employee sit at a desk all day reading through the material. Tours are great. No matter in which department the employee will work, provide a tour of all or at least some key departments and those that are appropriate (safety, security, or other considerations may preclude touring in some areas). The more the employee understands the scope of the entire organization's processes and not just those of his department, the more apt he is to feel a part of the entire organization and understand how his work and the work of his department contributes to company-wide operations. Show the employee a copy of your organizational chart so he can see how and where he fits in the bigger scheme of things.

Ease the paperwork burden. Each of us has likely experienced the overwhelming volume of paper and information you receive the first day on the job, from benefits (life, health, pension/401(k), STD, LTD) to payroll (timesheets, direct deposit, tax forms), and so much more. It may be helpful to provide all the information on Day One and then to have a rolling review over the next several days by which you can come back to the employee and review key topics; e.g., Day Two — collect completed Form I-9 and payroll/tax forms and answer related questions; Day Three — collect completed health/welfare/pension forms and answer related questions, etc.

Another process and tool that can be useful is a departmental orientation checklist. The expectations you have for all employees are covered in your broader NEO program. Certain and other expectations, however, may vary from department to department. Safety or security may be critical in one department, less so in others. Consider developing a departmental orientation checklist for each department to share and review with employees hired in a specific department. While the same checklist will likely be used by all managers working in the same department, the checklists may vary from department to department. Checklist items may include dress code; attendance and punctuality; opening and closing procedures; equipment/machinery use and maintenance; meal and rest periods; shifts; and more. This may be more difficult than you think. There is so much we take for granted when we come to work. To develop a checklist for your department, consider talking to one or two of your newest employees. Ask them what questions they had in their first day, week, and month that could have been better addressed. You may decide you need to drill down one more level and develop a checklist for various jobs within certain departments as the expectations listed above may also vary within a department for employees working in different jobs.

Job Shadowing, Mentoring, and On-the-Job Training

Whether your onboarding program is one week or one month, you will want to establish a method or process by which the new employee has a key contact for day-to-day interaction, learning, and feedback. Some companies have a formal on-the-job-training (OJT), buddy, or job shadowing program by which high performers may volunteer and are selected to serve as mentors to new employees. The new employee may shadow the mentor for the first week or so to learn the specifics of the new job related to procedures and processes. As with the NEO process that implements a departmental orientation checklist, a checklist for OJT is helpful as well. This can help ensure consistency in the training of new employees in the same job classification. While the output or productivity of the new employee will likely be lower during this period, the cost of lower productivity may be well offset by the avoidance of or subsequent reduction in errors that may result from a more fully informed and trained employee.

Where job shadowing is not feasible, some employers may still provide a mentor. The mentor, again, may be a more senior and top-performing employee to whom the new employee can go to ask questions or seek clarification about job processes or procedures. This process is less formal and likely will not include a checklist, but the person serves as a resource and key contact for the new employee to lend additional support during the initial learning curve.

Feedback

You can learn a lot about your onboarding process by including a formal mechanism by which the new employee and his supervisor can provide feedback. The supervisor, using both the onboarding and departmental orientation checklists, can ensure all areas, topics, and issues have been covered and can provide the new employee with feedback regarding his performance to date. Likewise, and just as important, the new employee can provide feedback to the company about the onboarding process. That feedback might be given to HR in lieu of the manager or supervisor to help ensure the employee feels completely comfortable sharing any concerns about the process or recommendations for improvement. Whatever structure you use, this can be done in a stop-start-continue format. That is, what should we stop including in our onboarding process because it did not work well or did not add value? What should we start including in our onboarding process that would add value? What should we continue to include in our onboarding process because it worked well? And, of course, asking the new employee for related feedback, such as: What portions of the onboarding process should we modify or fine tune to enhance the process?

A Few Words about Retention You can do a fabulous job of welcoming, orientating, and/or onboarding your employees. But don't stop there. Retaining your top performers has myriad benefits to an employer and its employees. High retention means lower turnover, which may reduce time and costs related to recruitment, selection, hiring, and training. Top performers may also help enhance employee relations and morale by serving as mentors and role models for employees who are not yet performing as well as they can. So how do you figure out how to keep these employees? Ask them! Sit down with them for a "stay interview" to find out what keeps them with your organization.

Human Resource Executive Online published an article in 2015 that addresses some common questions related to stay interviews to facilitate the goal on increasing retention.[6] Topics addressed include:

- When to conduct stay interviews.

- With whom stay interviews should be conducted (all or select employees).
- The value of stay interviews for organizations that conduct employee satisfaction surveys.
- Who should conduct the stay interview, HR or the manager.
- The value of stay versus exit interviews.
- Some common questions to include in stay interviews.

SHRM has on its website in the "Resources & Tools" section some common questions and answers available to SHRM members. They include:

- What do you look forward to when you come to work each day?
- What do you like most or least about working here?
- What keeps you working here?
- If you could change something about your job, what would that be?
- What would make your job more satisfying?
- How do you like to be recognized?
- What talents are not being used in your current role?
- What would you like to learn here?
- What motivates (or demotivates) you?
- What can I do to best support you?
- What can I do more of or less of as your manager?
- What might tempt you to leave?

No matter how, when, or with whom you conduct a stay interview, don't let the survey results sit on a shelf! Use them. Practically apply them to enhance your HR and employment policies, practices and programs.

Practical Tips

- Collaborate. A key to a successful onboarding program is collaborative development. Build your program with input from executive team members, department managers, front-line supervisors, human resources, and employees actually doing the work. You may be surprised by what you will hear is important to each group.

With this feedback, you can develop a well-rounded program that meets the needs of the entire organization, across all levels, and from a variety of perspectives.

• Give the big and little picture. It can be helpful to provide the new employee with a copy of the company's organizational chart and departmental chart if the roles within the department are not spelled out on the organizational chart. This way, the employee can see where he fits into the organization, and it can lead to a discussion about succession planning, career ladders, and more.

Foreword:
Practice Your Passion!

Throughout this book I have talked about federal, state, and local laws and regulations that impact HR and employment policies, practices, and procedures. So often we lament the administrative burdens and challenges these mandates and requirements impose upon those running the business. Yet so often when we hold up the mirror and ask, "What did I do to shape this law before it became law?" the answer is "nothing." Be the voice! No one knows better than you how a bill, a pending regulation, or agency guidance will impact your employment practices. Elected officials and appointed regulatory agency representatives need to hear your stories. They need to hear, learn, and understand how their proposals will impact your company's practices and your employees. Those stories will vary from company to company, industry to industry, and location to location.

You have read in this book some of the wonderful opportunities I have had over the years to speak at the federal and state levels. And I can tell you that one voice can make a difference. I remember more than a decade ago sitting in a committee of my Maryland General Assembly waiting to testify on a bill that would have made Maryland the second state to defeat the at-will nature of employment. The bill would have basically mirrored Montana's law and required Maryland employers to provide employees with written notice of the reason for involuntary termination. I and others testified, and the bill did not receive a favorable report and moved no further. The question I asked then and try to always ask is "why?" Why did this bill arise in the first place? In that case, it was the result of one constituent. The bill sponsor shared that one constituent contacted the representative's office with a story of having been fired but given no reason as to why he was fired. Whether that was true or not, it spurred this representative to sponsor the bill.

I find that the "Power of Why" opens the dialogue, enhances understanding, and finds paths to mutual agreement or at least an opportunity to find some common ground from which to develop legislation and regulation that better meets the needs of employers and employees.

Advocacy does not have to take a lot of time. It can be a phone call, an e-mail, or a written letter. It can be supplemented with written or oral testimony, visits to legislators' offices, and more. The challenge for some is overcoming not knowing what to say or how to say it.

I first dipped my toes into the advocacy pool in 1994. I happened to be researching the history of my state's workers' compensation law when I learned a bill was pending that would modify the existing law and create greater liability for employers. The bug bit me, and I was pretty hooked. I am not a legislative junkie. I have no desire to become a registered lobbyist or become a political candidate. I applaud those who do. But I do have a firm commitment and belief that our advocacy makes a difference. Do you have your doubts? Let me share a success story here.

You may recall that, in 2004, the federal executive, administrative and professional (EAP) regulations changed (see Chapter 6). At that time, Maryland was one of at least 18 states that had its own white-collar or EAP regulations. So I wrote to our state Department of Labor, Licensing and Regulation, asking that the existing state regulations be removed since the federal regulations had just been updated. Otherwise, employers in our state would have had to continue to conduct a dual analysis before being able to properly classify any employee as exempt. I received no direct response to my letter, but approximately six months later I happened to be perusing our state regulations and guess what I found? Our state regulations had been modified and simply referred to the federal regulations. Coincidence? Perhaps. But I like to think our efforts had some impact. Still not convinced?

This is a short story of advocacy in support of, as opposed to, legislation. In 2007 Maryland's highest court issued a decision that reversed long-standing precedent regarding an employer's obligation to pay out accrued, unused leave at termination. The case held that such leave must be paid out at termination. Our state agency then modified its rule and published the same interpretation on its website. In response, our Maryland SHRM State Council joined with our state chamber of commerce and others to find a sponsor for a bill that would return our state to where we were. We testified in support of legislation that provided that an employee would be required to pay out accrued, unused leave in accordance with its own written policy. Only where the employer failed to have a policy that was provided to employees at the time of hire would the employer be obligated to pay out all accrued, unused paid leave (exclusive of sick leave). The response was not only in our favor but the bill was tagged an "emergency bill," making it effective the date the governor signed it rather than the usual effective date of October 1.

Advocacy does work. It works in not only shaping important public policy but in our own professional development and in forging new connections and relationships that may last a lifetime. So, I share with you here some tips I have learned along the way and hope they might assist you in your advocacy efforts.

1. Find an issue — federal, state, or local — that resonates with you as it relates to your company's operations.

2. Network, network, network! Find an HR or business partner or a colleague who shares your concern, whether it's in favor of, or opposition to, pending reform.

3. Don't go it alone — Together, find an association or organization that can help you advance your position and advocate. This might be a U.S., state, or local chamber of commerce or a professional or trade association such as SHRM and your state council or local chapter.

4. Read the legislation, pending rule, guidance, or regulation. Develop talking points to address your concerns, e.g., the business reason you support or oppose the proposal.

5. Fiscal impact — if the matter is pending legislation, be sure to read the attached fiscal note. Understand the projected impact to your market, industry, and company. Powerful stories include those that detail the fiscal impact proposals may have on one business, particularly small employers and non-profit organizations.

6. Draft your letter and/or talking points. KISS is the concept here: Keep it short and sweet. Legislators and appointed officials are no less busy than we are. Give them the nutshell version focusing on the impact to your employees and your company.

7. Make the ask — Like any good salesman, close your "sale" by asking for a vote that mirrors your position.

8. Follow up! Let the legislators or appointed officials know that you will be watching for the requested vote or action. Then do so. And send a letter or e-mail or make a quick call giving them thanks when they do and sharing your regret when they do not.

9. Maintain the relationship — Whether the legislator or elected official took the action you requested or not, suggest that you look forward to working with him or her in the future and remain available to serve as a resource in the future.

10. Pay it forward — A successful advocate grows advocacy. Find another colleague and offer to partner with them in the future to support these advocacy efforts.

Appendix.
Pre-Termination Checklist

Item	Description	Yes	No
Forewarning	Do you have documentation that shows what, how, and when you informed the employee of the expectations that are not currently met?		
Evidence	Do you have evidence to back up your position, such as: (1) the employee's own admission, (2) witnesses, or (3) tangible evidence?		
Proper Investigation	Prior to making your final decision, have you heard the employee's side of the story and interviewed potential witnesses?		
Lack of Discrimination	Have you treated other employees who have been similarly situated the same? If not, is there a reason for treating this employee differently that is job-related and consistent with business necessity?		
Penalty Meets the Offense	Is it reasonable to think there is any action you could take, other than termination, to correct the employee's behavior (e.g., have you documented previous coaching, counseling, and corrective action)?		
Policy versus Practice	Is termination consistent with your policy and your past practice? If not, see "Lack of Discrimination," above.		
Demographics	Does this termination follow any particular trend in the department, business unit, or organization at large related to protected status such as age, race, or sex? If yes, do you know why?		
Recent Events	Has this employee recently engaged in any protected activity, such as expressing concerns about wages, hours, or conditions of employment or had any occurrence outside the usual course of business such as filing a workers' compensation claim, seeking FMLA leave, or informing you of a medical condition such as pregnancy?		

Endnotes

Chapter 1

[1] [(Number of days absent in a month) / (average number of employees during month) x (number of workdays)] x 100. See SHRM's Tools and Resources, https://www.shrm.org/resourcesandtools/tools-and-samples/pages/spreadsheets.aspx

[2] Montana Code Annotated § 39-2-904 (FindLaw website), http://codes.findlaw.com/mt/title-39-labor/mt-code-ann-sect-39-2-904.html

[3] SHRM Tools and Resources, https://www.shrm.org/resourcesandtools/tools-and-samples/pages/spreadsheets.aspx

[4] Waivers of ADEA Claims, https://www.eeoc.gov/policy/docs/qanda_severance-agreements.html#IV

[5] Waivers of ADEA Claims, https://www.eeoc.gov/policy/docs/qanda_severance-agreements.html#B

[6] Defend Trade Secrets Act of 2016, https://www.congress.gov/114/plaws/publ153/PLAW-114publ153.pdf

Chapter 2

[1] "Incentive Pay Schemes Can Affect Employee Well-Being," Phys.org (2017), https://phys.org/news/2017-01-incentive-schemes-affect-employee-well-being.html

[2] "Is It Time to Put the Performance Review on a PIP?" Dori Meinert, *HR Magazine* (2015), https://www.shrm.org/hr-today/news/hr-magazine/Pages/0415-qualitative-performance-reviews.aspx

3 "Employers Seek Better Approaches to Pay for Performance," Stephen Miller, CEBS, SHRM Online (2016), https://www.shrm.org/ResourcesAndTools/hr-topics/compensation/pages/better-pay-for-performance.aspx

4 "Managing Employee Performance," SHRM Online Toolkits (2015), https://www.shrm.org/resourcesandtools/tools-and-samples/toolkits/pages/managingemployeeperformance.aspx

5 "Improving Performance Evaluations Using Calibration," Stephen Miller, CEBS, SHRM Online (2014), https://www.shrm.org/resourcesandtools/hr-topics/compensation/pages/calibration-sessions.aspx

6 *Global Performance Management Survey Report*, Executive Summary (2013), Mercer, https://www.mercer.com/content/dam/mercer/attachments/global/Talent/Assess-BrochurePerfMgmt.pdf

7 *The Peter Principle: Why Things Always Go Wrong*, Laurence J. Peter and Raymond Hill (New York: Morrow, 1969). Also see "Peter Principle" at https://en.wikipedia.org/wiki/Peter_principle

Chapter 3

1 http://thinkexist.com/quotes/theodore_isaac_rubin/

2 http://www.acronymfinder.com/SMART.html

3 *Leadership and the One Minute Manager,* p. 38, Ken Blanchard (New York: Morrow, 1985). For more information on the Revised and Updated edition, see https://www.kenblanchard.com/Store/Books/Leadership-and-the-One-Minute-Manager

4 "Are You a Seagull Manager?" Travis Bradbury, Forbes Online (2016), https://www.forbes.com/sites/travisbradberry/2016/05/04/how-seagull-managers-make-everyone-miserable/#172c77a36d54

5 "Why a 'Seagull Manager' Might Be the Worst Kind of Manager" Sharon Zeev, *CEO Magazine* (2016), http://www.theceomagazine.com/business/why-a-seagull-manager-might-be-the-worst-kind-of-manager/

6 *Zapp! The Lightning of Empowerment,* William Byham, Ph.D. (New York, Ballantine Books, 1997). For more information, see https://

www.amazon.com/Zapp-Lightning-Empowerment-Productivity-
Satisfaction/dp/0449002829/ref=sr_1_1?s=books&ie=UTF8&qid=
1488138638&sr=1-1&keywords=zapp+the+lightning+of+empower
ment

[7] *Who Moved My Cheese?* Spencer Johnson, M.D. (New York, G.P. Putnam's Sons, 1998). For more information, see https://www.amazon.com/Who-Moved-My-Cheese-Amazing/dp/0399144463/ref=sr_1_1?s=books&ie=UTF8&qid=1488138722&sr=1-1&keywords=who+moved+my+cheese

[8] "Learning Theories/Adult Learning Theories," Wikibooks, https://en.wikibooks.org/wiki/Learning_Theories/Adult_Learning_Theories

[9] "Pareto Principle," Wikipedia, https://en.wikipedia.org/wiki/Pareto_principle

[10] "Josh Billings," Brainy Quote, https://www.brainyquote.com/quotes/quotes/j/joshbillin100690.html

[11] *Connick v. Myers*, 461 U.S. 138 (1983). For more information, see https://supreme.justia.com/cases/federal/us/461/138/case.html

Chapter 4

[1] "The ADA Turns 25," EEOC website, https://www.eeoc.gov/eeoc/history/ada25th/index.cfm

[2] Code of Federal Regulations, Title 29, 1630.2, https://www.gpo.gov/fdsys/pkg/CFR-2011-title29-vol4/xml/CFR-2011-title29-vol4-part1630.xml

[3] "Employer-Provided Leave and the Americans with Disabilities Act" (2016), EEOC website, https://www.eeoc.gov/eeoc/publications/ada-leave.cfm

[4] "Sears, Roebuck to Pay $6.2 Million for Disability Bias" (2009), EEOC website, https://www.eeoc.gov/eeoc/newsroom/release/archive/9-29-09.html

[5] "Facts About the Americans with Disabilities Act," EEOC website, https://www.eeoc.gov/eeoc/publications/fs-ada.cfm

[6] "Final Rule on Employer Wellness Programs and Title I of the Americans with Disabilities Act" (2016), EEOC website, https://www.eeoc.gov/laws/regulations/qanda-ada-wellness-final-rule.cfm

[7] "Sample Notice for Employer-Sponsored Wellness Programs" (2016), EEOC website, https://www.eeoc.gov/laws/regulations/ada-wellness-notice.cfm

[8] "Enforcement Guidance on Pregnancy Discrimination and Related Issues," EEOC website, https://www.eeoc.gov/laws/guidance/pregnancy_guidance.cfm

[9] *Young v. United Parcel Service, Inc.* (2014), https://www.supremecourt.gov/opinions/14pdf/12-1226_k5fl.pdf

[10] Id. at 1354-55, https://www.supremecourt.gov/opinions/14pdf/12-1226_k5fl.pdf

[11] "Enforcement Guidances and Related Documents," EEOC website, https://www.eeoc.gov/laws/guidance/enforcement_guidance.cfm

[12] "Fiscal Year Data for Wage and Hour Division," DOL website, https://www.dol.gov/whd/data/datatables.htm

[13] "The Employee's Guide to the Family and Medical Leave Act" (2015), DOL website, https://www.dol.gov/whd/fmla/employeeguide.pdf

[14] Code of Federal Regulations, Title 29, 825.300(a)(2), https://www.gpo.gov/fdsys/granule/CFR-2011-title29-vol3/CFR-2011-title29-vol3-sec825-300 15 "Administrator's Interpretation 2013-1" (2013), DOL website, https://www.dol.gov/WHD/opinion/adminIntrprtn/FMLA/2013/FMLAAI2013_1.htm

[16] Code of Federal Regulations, Title 29, 825.113(d), https://www.gpo.gov/fdsys/granule/CFR-2012-title29-vol3/CFR-2012-title29-vol3-sec825-113

[17] USERRA Training, DOL website, https://www.dol.gov/vets/programs/userra/onlinetraining.htm

[18] "State Laws on Voting Rights/Time Off to Vote" (2017), Workplace Fairness website, http://www.workplacefairness.org/voting-rights-time-off-work

[19] Healthy Families Act (2015), GovTrack website, https://www.govtrack.us/congress/bills/114/s497

20 "Current Sick Days Laws" (2016), Support Paid Sick Days website, http://www.paidsickdays.org/research-resources/current-sick-days-laws.html

Chapter 5

1 "The Importance of Employee Engagement," Dale Carnegie website, http://www.dalecarnegie.com/employee-engagement/engaged-employees-infographic/

2 "Using Employee Engagement to Build a Diverse Workforce," Rebecca Riffkin and Jim Harter (2016), Gallup website, http://www.gallup.com/opinion/gallup/190103/using-employee-engagement-build-diverse-workforce.aspx

3 "The Role of Diversity Practices and Inclusion in Promoting Trust and Employee Engagement" (2015), Deloitte website, https://www2.deloitte.com/au/en/pages/human-capital/articles/role-diversity-practices-inclusion-trust-employee-engagement.html

4 "Harassment," EEOC website, https://www.eeoc.gov/laws/types/harassment.cfm

5 "Sexual Harassment," EEOC website, https://www.eeoc.gov/laws/types/sexual_harassment.cfm

6 Workplace Bullying Survey (2014), Workplace Bullying Institute website, http://www.workplacebullying.org/wbiresearch/wbi-2014-us-survey/

7 2104 WBI U.S. Workplace Bullying Survey (2014), Gary Namie, WBI website, http://workplacebullying.org/multi/pdf/WBI-2014-US-Survey.pdf

8 "Enforcement Guidance on Retaliation and Related Issues," EEOC website, https://www.eeoc.gov/laws/guidance/retaliation-guidance.cfm

9 "Employee's Right to Report Injuries and Illnesses Free from Retaliation" (2016), OSHA website, https://www.osha.gov/recordkeeping/modernization_guidance.html

10 "Fact Sheet: Retaliation Based on Exercise of Workplace Rights is Unlawful" (2016), Department of Labor website, https://www.dol.

gov/dol/fact-sheet/immigration/RetaliationBasedExerciseWorkplac-eRightsUnlawful.htm

Chapter 6

[1] "President Obama's FY 2017 Budget Proposal" (2016), The Coalition to Promote Independent Entrepreneurs website, http://www.iecoalition.org/federal-news/president-obamas-fy-2017-budget-proposal/

[2] "Misclassification of Employees as Independent Contractors," Department of Labor website, https://www.dol.gov/whd/workers/misclassification/

[3] "Fact Sheet 13: Am I an Employee? Employment Relationship Under the Fair Labor Standards Act" (2014), DOL website, https://www.dol.gov/whd/regs/compliance/whdfs13.htm

[4] DOL website, "Administrator's Interpretation No. 2015-1" (2015), DOL website, https://www.dol.gov/whd/workers/misclassification/AI-2015_1.htm

[5] "Independent Contractor or Employee," Publication 1779, Rev. 3-2012, IRS website, https://www.irs.gov/pub/irs-pdf/p1779.pdf

[6] "Fact Sheet #71: Internship Programs Under The Fair Labor Standards Act" (2010), DOL website, https://www.dol.gov/whd/regs/compliance/whdfs71.pdf

[7] Montana Code Annotated § 39-2-901, FindLaw website, http://codes.findlaw.com/mt/title-39-labor/mt-code-ann-sect-39-2-901.html

[8] Code of Federal Regulations, Title 29, 541.602, Government Publishing website, https://www.gpo.gov/fdsys/pkg/CFR-2016-title29-vol3/pdf/CFR-2016-title29-vol3-sec541-602.pdf

[9] "Opinion Letters: Fair Labor Standards Act" (2009), DOL website, https://www.dol.gov/whd/opinion/flsa.htm

[10] Id.

[11] "Fact Sheet 17B Exemption for Executive Employees Under the Fair Labor Standards Act" (2008), DOL website, https://www.dol.gov/whd/overtime/fs17b_executive.pdf

12 "Fact Sheet #17C: Exemption for Administrative Employees Under the Fair Labor Standards Act" (2008), DOL website, https://www.dol. gov/whd/overtime/fs17c_administrative.pdf

13 "Fact Sheet #17D: Exemption for Professional Employees Under the Fair Labor Standards Act" (2008), DOL website, https://www.dol. gov/whd/overtime/fs17d_professional.pdf

Chapter 7

1 Code of Federal Regulations, Title 29, 541.603(d), GPO website, https://www.gpo.gov/fdsys/pkg/CFR-2016-title29-vol3/pdf/CFR-2016-title29-vol3-sec541-603.pdf

2 "Model Salary Basis Policy," DOL website, https://www.dol.gov/whd/ regs/compliance/overtime/modelPolicy_PF.htm

3 "Enforcement Guidance on National Origin Discrimination," EEOC website, https://www.eeoc.gov/laws/guidance/national-origin-guidance.cfm

4 "Prohibited Employment Policies/Practices," EEOC website, https:// www.eeoc.gov/laws/practices/

5 "General Counsel Memos," National Labor Relations Board website, https://www.nlrb.gov/reports-guidance/general-counsel-memos

6 "The NLRB and Social Media," NLRB website, https://www.nlrb.gov/ news-outreach/fact-sheets/nlrb-and-social-media

Chapter 8

1 "Onboarding New Employees: Maximizing Success," Talya N. Bauer, Ph.D., SHRM Online, https://www.shrm.org/foundation/ourwork/ initiatives/resources-from-past-initiatives/Documents/Onboarding%20New%20Employees.pdf

2 "How to Get Employee Onboarding Right" (2015), Maren Hogan, Forbes website, https://www.forbes.com/sites/theyec/2015/05/29/ how-to-get-employee-onboarding-right/#454b9087407b

3 "Worldwide 13% of Employees Are Engaged at Work" (2013), Steve Crabtree, Gallup website, http://www.gallup.com/poll/165269/ worldwide-employees-engaged-work.aspx

[4] "Majority of U.S. Employees Not Engaged Despite Gains in 2014" (2015), Amy Adkins, Gallup website, http://www.gallup.com/poll/181289/majority-employees-not-engaged-despite-gains-2014.aspx

[5] "Employee Engagement in U.S. Stagnant in 2015" (2015), Amy Adkins, Gallup website, http://www.gallup.com/poll/188144/employee-engagement-stagnant-2015.aspx

[6] "The Stay Interview" (2015), HR Executive website, http://www.hreonline.com/HRE/view/story.jhtml?id=534358694

Index

Acknowledgements

To Mark — In the six years since the first edition of this book was published, just as in the 22 years since we met before that, your support has never wavered. Thank you for your constant trust, confidence, support, and love. I absolutely could not have done this without you.

To Mom and Dad — you laid the foundation that made this book (and any success I might humbly say I have) possible. Thank you for teaching me the value of a strong work ethic, kindness, and honor.

To Janet — You left this life in 2016. You will continue to inspire me. Your friend in eternity.

About the Author

Christine V. Walters, MAS, JD, SPHR, has nearly 25 years of combined experience in HR administration, management, employment law practice, and teaching. She has been engaged as an expert witness, and testified before the U.S. Congress, state legislative committees, and federal administrative agencies. Walters has been interviewed and quoted in a variety of media, including television, radio, and print media.

Throughout her career, Walters has been honored with awards and accolades, including:

- Small Business of the Year Award — B/W Corridor Chamber of Commerce, April 2010
- Nominee — Daily Record's "Leadership in Law" Award, 2009
- Finalist — Maryland Chamber of Commerce Small Business of the Year Award, 2009
- President's Award — B/W Corridor Chamber of Commerce, 2003
- Capitol Award — Society for Human Resource Management (SHRM), 2002
- Outstanding Leadership Award — American Society for Healthcare Human Resource Administration (ASHHRA), 1997
- Best Practices Award — ASHHRA, 1996

Walters has presented at national, regional, and state conferences across the country, including the Society for Human Resource Management (SHRM), Employment Management Association (EMA), the American Physical Therapy Association, College and University Personnel Association, Credit Union National Association, and more.

Today, Walters serves as an independent consultant doing business as FiveL Company, *Helping Leaders Limit Their Liability by Learning the Law*[SM], providing proactive guidance, training programs, education, and counsel on employment and HR issues, policies, procedures, and practices for clients across the country and in a variety of industries. She was also an adjunct faculty member of the Johns Hopkins University, teaching a variety of courses in the graduate, undergraduate, and certification level programs from 1999 through 2006.

Walters demonstrates her commitment to supporting and advancing the needs and interests of the business community and HR profession by serving in a variety of volunteer leadership roles, including and not limited to:

- Secretary — Maryland SHRM State Council
- Executive and HR Committees — Carroll County Chamber of Commerce
- President, Carroll County SHRM
- Editorial Advisory Board Member — Thompson Publishing's FMLA Handbook
- Board Member — Maryland Chamber of Commerce
- Board Member — Hunt Valley Business Forum
- Advisory Board Member — McDaniel College, Graduate Program in Human Resources
- Former Member — SHRM's Legislative Action and Employee Relations Committees

Walters is licensed to practice law in the state of Maryland.

Additional
SHRM-Published Books

View from the Top: Leveraging Human and Organization Capital to Create Value
Richard L. Antoine, Libby Sartain, Dave Ulrich, Patrick M. Wright

California Employment Law: An Employer's Guide, Revised & Updated for 2017
James J. McDonald, Jr.

101 Sample Write-ups for Documenting Employee Performance Problems: A Guide to Progressive Discipline & Termination, Third Edition
Paul Falcone

Developing Business Acumen
SHRM Competency Series: Making an Impact in Small Business HR
Jennifer Currence

Applying Critical Evaluation
SHRM Competency Series: Making an Impact in Small Business HR
Jennifer Currence

Touching People's Lives: Leaders' Sorrow or Joy
Michael R. Losey

Defining HR Success: 9 Critical Competencies for HR Professionals
Kari R. Strobel, James N. Kurtessis, Debra J. Cohen, and Alexander Alonso

HR on Purpose: Developing Deliberate People Passion
Steve Browne

A Manager's Guide to Developing Competencies in HR Staff
Phyllis G. Hartman

Tips and Tools for Improving Proficiency in Your Reports
Phyllis G. Hartman

Developing Proficiency in HR: 7 Self-Directed Activities for HR Professionals
Debra J. Cohen

Manager Onboarding: 5 Steps for Setting New Leaders Up for Success
Sharlyn Lauby

Destination Innovation: HR's Role in Charting the Course
Patricia M. Buhler

Got a Solution? HR Approaches to 5 Common and Persistent Business Problems
Dale J. Dwyer & Sheri A. Caldwell

HR's Greatest Challenge: Driving the C-Suite to Improve Employee Engagement and Retention
Richard P. Finnegan

Business-Focused HR: 11 Processes to Drive Results
Shane S. Douthitt & Scott P. Mondore

Proving the Value of HR: How and Why to Measure ROI, Second Edition
Jack J. Phillips & Patricia Pulliam Phillips

SHRM Books Approved for Recertification Credit

Aligning HR & Business Strategy/Holbeche, 9780750680172 (2009)

Becoming the Evidence-Based Manager/Latham, 9780891063988 (2009)

Being Global/Cabrera, 9781422183229 (2012)

Best Practices in Succession Planning/Linkage, 9780787985790 (2007)

Calculating Success/Hoffmann, 9781422166390 (2012)

Collaborate/Sanker, 9781118114728 (2012)

Deep Dive/Horwath, 9781929774821 (2009)

Effective HR Management/Lawler, 9780804776875 (2012)

Emotional Intelligence/Bradbury, 9780974320625 (2009)

Employee Engagement/Carbonara, 9780071799508 (2012)

From Hello to Goodbye/Walters, 978158644447 (2017)

Handbook for Strategic HR/Vogelsang, 9780814432495 (2012)

Hidden Drivers of Success/Schiemann, 9781586443337 (2013)

HR at Your Service/Latham, 9781586442477 (2012)

HR Transformation/Ulrich, 9780071638708 (2009)

Lean HR/Lay, 9781481914208 (2013)

Manager 3.0/Karsh, 9780814432891 (2013)

Managing Employee Turnover/Allen, 9781606493403 (2012)

Managing the Global Workforce/Caliguri, 9781405107327 (2010)

Managing the Mobile Workforce/Clemons, 9780071742207 (2010)

Managing Older Workers/Cappelli, 9781422131657 (2010)

Multipliers/Wiseman, 9780061964398 (2010)

Negotiation at Work/Asherman, 9780814431900 (2012)

Nine Minutes on Monday/Robbins, 9780071801980 (2012)

One Strategy/Sinofsky, 9780470560457 (2009)

People Analytics/Waber, 9780133158311 (2013)

Performance Appraisal Tool Kit/Falcone, 9780814432631 (2013)

Point Counterpoint/Tavis, 9781586442767 (2012)

Practices for Engaging the 21st Century Workforce/Castellano, 9780133086379 (2013)

Proving the Value of HR/Phillips, 9781586442880 (2012)

Reality-Based Leadership/Wakeman, 9780470613504 (2010)

Social Media Strategies/Golden, 9780470633106 (2010)

Talent, Transformations, and Triple Bottom Line/Savitz, 9781118140970 (2013)

The Big Book of HR/Mitchell, 9781601631893 (2012)

The Crowdsourced Performance Review/Mosley, 9780071817981 (2013)

The Definitive Guide to HR Communications/Davis, 9780137061433 (2011)

The e-HR Advantage/Waddill, 9781904838340 (2011)

The Employee Engagement Mindset/Clark, 9780071788298 (2012)

The Global Challenge/Evans, 9780073530376 (2010)

The Global Tango/Trompenaars, 9780071761154 (2010)

The HR Answer Book/Smith, 9780814417171 (2011)

The Manager's Guide to HR/Muller, 9780814433027 (2013)

The Power of Appreciative Inquiry/Whitney, 9781605093284 (2010)

Transformative HR/Boudreau, 9781118036044 (2011)

What If? Short Stories to Spark Diversity Dialogue/Robbins, 9780891062752 (2008)

What Is Global Leadership?/Gundling, 9781904838234 (2011)

Winning the War for Talent/Johnson, 9780730311553 (2011)